THE EDUCATION OF A TEACHER

THE EDUCATION OF A TEACHER

Including Dirty Books and Pointed Looks

SUSAN VAN KIRK

iUniverse, Inc.
New York Bloomington

The Education of a Teacher
Including Dirty Books and Pointed Looks

Copyright © 2010 by Brakelight, LLC

All rights reserved. No part of this book may be used or reproduced by any means, graphic, electronic, or mechanical, including photocopying, recording, taping or by any information storage retrieval system without the written permission of the publisher except in the case of brief quotations embodied in critical articles and reviews.

Cover Design by Darren Jackson
Cover Photo by Dr. James DeYoung
Author Photo by Portraits by Buff

iUniverse books may be ordered through booksellers or by contacting:

iUniverse
1663 Liberty Drive
Bloomington, IN 47403
www.iuniverse.com
1-800-Authors (1-800-288-4677)

Because of the dynamic nature of the Internet, any Web addresses or links contained in this book may have changed since publication and may no longer be valid. The views expressed in this work are solely those of the author and do not necessarily reflect the views of the publisher, and the publisher hereby disclaims any responsibility for them.

ISBN: 978-1-4502-5096-2 (sc)
ISBN: 978-1-4502-5098-6 (dj)
ISBN: 978-1-4502-5097-9 (ebk)

Library of Congress Control Number: 2010912023

Printed in the United States of America

iUniverse rev. date: 08/18/2010

For my parents, who were always proud that I was a teacher, for my amazing children and grandchildren, and for Greg, who always said, "Of course you can do this." And in loving memory of my beautiful and clever granddaughter, Gwendolyn Grace Anderson Van Kirk.

Contents

Preface 1

Part I The Age of Aquarius (Late 1960s and the 1970s)

Chapter One You Are Now Entering the Maple City 9

Chapter Two War and Remembrance 19

Chapter Three Early Days: Chaos and Confusion 28

Chapter Four "Hi. I'm Barb. I Sneeze." 41

Chapter Five A Winter Tale 57

Chapter Six Past Tense, Future Perfect 74

Chapter Seven Great Expectations 81

Part II The Middle Years (1980s)

Chapter Eight Sabrina Fair 99

Chapter Nine And the Walls Came Tumbling Down 104

Chapter Ten Transitions 123

Chapter Eleven Mr. Detroit 141

Chapter Twelve The Boy Who Dreamed He Could Run 159

Part III Elder Stateswoman (1990s)

Chapter Thirteen The Mirror of His High School Eyes 177

Chapter Fourteen Mr. Vonnegut and Me 182

Chapter Fifteen Postscript (2008) Rockin' Out 242

Acknowledgments 249

Permissions and Legal Releases 251

Preface

In spring 2004, Kurt Carlson, a student in my educational foundations class at Monmouth College, stopped after class and said, "You should put that story you told us today into writing. It's inspirational, and people who want to be teachers should read it." I tucked his thought away until I noticed a trend in my college student class evaluations: "Tell us more stories about what it's like to teach in a real classroom." I had used three stories during the semester, and each examined issues that we were discussing. After much thought, I decided to try to put those stories and others into writing. And so, Kurt Carlson, here is your book.

The first story I wrote, "Class Reunions," appears in this collection as "War and Remembrance." I sent it to *Teacher Magazine,* hoping they might publish it, and they did so immediately. I was encouraged. Once it was published, I decided to do a collection of stories, and I began to consider four possible audiences for my book. Now that this six-year undertaking is completed, I'd like to add a few words about those audiences, as well as the classrooms I left. Both were instrumental in the writing of this memoir.

The first audience I imagined was pre-service teachers: people like Kurt Carlson and the other students I instructed at Monmouth College. They reminded me that these education stories were examples of social issues, ethics, fears, inspirations, and joys that define a life in classrooms. College students desire so much more than benchmarks and standardized testing knowledge. They want to know about the messy side of teaching where human beings interact. Every day teachers go into public schools and experience exhaustion, frustration, and pain, but they also receive joy and love, and feel that they are doing terribly important work in the world. Salaries certainly don't keep them there.

These pre-service teachers need to know that, like life, teaching involves daily creative tensions. Should I do this or should I do that? Should I step in or should I pull out? Teachers continually experience a range of actions between hesitation to act, thoughtful decision-making, and intuitive, quick, reaction. If they teach, they will learn to tread a path through these ambiguities and to discover that every situation is completely different from the one before. Because teaching is a life among human beings who interact in wildly different configurations, teachers never have a template that provides a solution to every possibility. These stories certainly reflect that truth and also provide ethical, debatable, and realistic examples.

The second readers I could imagine for this story collection were teachers already in the field, especially the younger ones. They seem glad to be reminded of the important work they are doing in a society that rarely rewards them. They recognize, too, the idea that teachers are shaped and matured by their early years in classrooms so that they gain a stronger sense of themselves. I arranged the stories in this book chronologically for exactly that reason. I began teaching as a twenty-one-year-old who thought she had all the answers. Like about 50 percent of first-year teachers who consider quitting, I, too, thought about leaving. But I found my "sea legs" and fell in love with the voyage I had chosen for the rest of my life. I gained valuable experience and maturity that directed my actions in the later stories from my career.

My children and grandchildren are my third audience. My children lived through many of these years but didn't know the human dramas that were part of their mother's workday. Now they will. Without the encouragement of Mike, Jennifer, and Steve, I could not have written this memoir. Like many baby boomers, I retired from public school teaching just as my grandchildren were born. They are too young to know their grandmother as a teacher, but through these pages they will discover who she was in that life. You can't hide who you are when you write, and you certainly can't hide your beliefs when you teach. Recently, the dean of Monmouth College, Jane Jakoubek, was discussing grading, but in a broader sense, she was defining something far greater when she wrote these words in a communication to the faculty: "There is something in the heart of a teacher that connects the principles by which one lives and the principles by which one grades. I remember teachers who used the standard of 'justice' in all things; I remember teachers who extended 'grace' as well. I learned different but equally important lessons from each of them. We cannot teach well except out of the core of who we are and what we believe."

And there is a fourth group I imagined as I wrote, to whom I owe great thanks: those four thousand-plus students who went through my classrooms and taught me both who I was and how I should teach. Many of them helped in the writing of this book. Between phone calls, emails, and personal visits, they gently corrected my memory, shared great details of their lives and their own memories, and pushed me to finish this book. It was a joy to share this journey with them. They were the kind critics and enthusiastic encouragers. For them and the years that I cherished in their midst, I included a reminder of the maroon and gold school colors and the "Zippers."

The high school classroom I left also informed my writing. Long before the No Child Left Behind (NCLB) law took over the way public school teachers teach, I remember classrooms where learning was taking place with very little standardized testing. Teachers were able to explore worlds without boundaries because they didn't have to cut back their endeavors in order to teach to The Test. The arts flourished because weeks were not lost to The Test. These stories describe such a world, and not a single story in this collection describes a day of standardized testing. I believe it is instructive to remember such a time before politicians looked for simple, black-and-white numbers to describe whether schools were "working." Those lawmakers failed—as is often the case—to allocate money to cash-strapped schools so those schools could pay millions to buy tests and test evaluations in order to adhere to the law. That was the world I left when I retired from the public schools; unfortunately, that is the world my college students are inheriting. I felt it was important to give the future a glimpse of that pre-NCLB world. If educational policy history is any indication, with its ebb and flow of trends, NCLB too will pass.

The school stories that make the news today are tales of scandals, violence, or teacher abuse. Such stories are often translated into films like *Stand and Deliver*, *Dangerous Minds*, and *Freedom Writers*. These are dramatic stories of schools in urban areas that have serious problems with violence.

However, thousands of schools in small towns all over this country have gripping stories about the interplay among school, community, teachers, parents, and students. School systems such as Monmouth District 38 reflect the town that supports them. Arriving in this community, I became deeply entrenched in a small town that had severe economic problems and an unusually high percentage of children from low socio-economic homes. These demographics resulted in problems that spilled over into the schools. Many stories in this collection reflect those harsh realities: unplanned pregnancies, drug abuse, and domestic violence. However, those are not the only realities in a teacher's life. I also included stories that are humorous, because you can never discount the entertainment value of students.

A brief word about privacy issues—I have changed the actual names of people in chapters six, seven, ten, and fourteen. In chapter fourteen, the newspaper coverage included the actual names of people who were part of that story. However, to keep those names consistent with the chapter, I also changed them in the newspaper coverage.

This collection tells not simply the stories of a teacher but it also reflects a compilation of events that could happen anywhere. Change the name of the town, school, and students, and you will find such truths in places other than tiny Monmouth, Illinois. And, as with all universal truths, this one town, in this one place, with these students, and this school, inform the truth of my one teaching life.

Part I

The Age of Aquarius
(Late 1960s and the 1970s)

Chapter One

You Are Now Entering the Maple City

I never imagined that I could get lost trying to find the college library in a tiny town of ten thousand souls known as the Maple City. It was the year 1963, my junior year in high school, when I first drove into the small town of Monmouth, located in west central Illinois, twenty miles from the Mississippi River.

The city square—which was actually a circle—was bisected by Main Street going north and south and by Broadway to the east and west. Coming in from the north, I turned off the square going west. Once again I found myself in corn and bean fields, heading out

The city square/circle

of town without a college in sight and no large buildings other than grain bins. So I backtracked and drove onto the square/circle, this time turning south. I passed a number of stores, the Rivoli Theatre, and a fire station, but once again I ended up back in the corn fields. No college.

Did I stop and ask directions? Why would I do that? In a town that had streets named A Street, B Street, C Street, and First and Second avenues, how could a person get lost? So I tried driving east from the square/circle and eventually discovered college buildings.

Heading south past a Maple City Dairy truck

I had no idea, as a sixteen-year-old, that I was passing the very locations that would become landmarks in my future life. During my aimless, where-is-that-college journey, I drove by three houses on Broadway where I would live, and I passed within a block of the high school where I'd spend thirty-four years of my life. On my trip back to the square from the west end of town, I ventured by a Roman Catholic church whose manger scene would lose a Wise Man to the clutches of one of my mischievous future students. Near that church, the Maple City Dairy would provide mouth-watering peach ice cream when I was pregnant with my daughter, and on warm summer nights my son would ride his tricycle to the dairy while I walked along behind. It would be a half block from our second home. I didn't realize then that the dairy's owner,

House on far right was ours; high school is upper center right behind the church steeple; Maple City Dairy is white building slightly up left of center.

the Petersen family, would leave an enduring imprint on my heart. Driving east from the square, I passed the Critser & Stansell law offices, owned by the parents of two of my early students who would come into my thoughts in astonishing ways. I finally found the Monmouth College library by accessing the campus from East Broadway and happily lost myself in research for a Civil War paper I was writing on the Underground Railroad. After my sojourn at the library, I drove east again, passing Benner's grocery store—later to be called Giant's—which would be the hilarious scene of my reunion so many years later with another student, Jack Harvey. Leaving town I noticed a sign that announced a local hospital where the ambulance would take one of my students after she had a brush with death in my classroom. So many places and people from Monmouth would become a part of me. But now, in 1963, they were all in my future, and I had to finish high school and college before I could discover this town again.

I moved to Monmouth in the summer of 1968, after graduating from college and getting married, to begin my first teaching job because my husband was already teaching nearby. I talked my way into a job teaching English and speech and directing plays at Monmouth High School. As a history major/ English minor in college, I had multiple hours of theatre work, so I assured George Pape, the high school principal, that I could teach what he needed, and he hired me. I felt he had made a wise decision, of course.

Monmouth High School

The first year I taught at MHS, I also directed the play *Our Town* by Thornton Wilder. Wilder's narrator, the Stage Manager, explained that knowing about our town involved economics, social issues, and politics. The same was true of my understanding of Monmouth.

Growing up in Galesburg, fifteen miles to the east, I knew nothing about the farming industry—I considered myself a "city girl"—and Monmouth's economy was based on agriculture. Now I realize that growing up in a town of thirty-eight thousand isn't exactly the definition of a "city girl," but you have to understand that I hadn't done much traveling. Despite driving by cornfields all my life, I didn't know a combine from a cultivator, and my liberal arts education hadn't included agriculture. In Monmouth, that sector supported three banks, a savings and loan, a farm credit agency, three implement dealers and an implement manufacturer, feed and grain dealers, a livestock sales barn, a frozen food locker, and a major farm supply retailer called Brown, Lynch, Scott. While I was one generation removed from my mother's farm family, I did know luscious crops of corn and beans when I saw them. And, proud of myself, I even recognized the John Deere logo. That was, however, the sum total of my agricultural knowledge.

As for industry, the town boasted several businesses. A pottery, a boat manufacturing company, a meat-packing plant, and a dog food manufacturer were the chief industries in the town. In fact, a huge tower on the south side of town would always be known as the "Wells elevator," a lasting symbol of the Wells dog food company.

Like the last act in Thornton Wilder's play, families who were early founders inhabited the local cemeteries, and their descendants still lived in the area. The names on the tombstones memorialized people who had migrated to the Midwest to start both a college and a town. Many of their descendants would occupy desks in my classroom.

The context of my future students' lives seemed more like that of the 1950s. Family life in Monmouth revolved around the homes, the churches, and the schools. My earliest students grew up in a town where kids had paper routes to earn spending money, rode bikes or walked to school by themselves, played outside all day without parental worry or Amber alerts, and had moms at home to fix lunch. At night they joined in games of kick-the-can, and on special days, like the Fourth of July, they attended patriotic parades and ceremonies. By the time I drove into town to begin my job, twenty churches, representing fourteen denominations, graced the various streets. Those churches provided opportunities for kids and families in youth groups, sports teams, and scouting.

I felt I had moved onto the set of *The Adventures of Ozzie and Harriet* television show.

On the evening news, the families of Monmouth watched reports of the Vietnam War and worried about their older sons or brothers. They witnessed protests on the local college campus, voted largely conservative Republican, and just shook their heads at those protesting hippies on the news. Churches, banks, and gas stations dominated the choice corners of town, with bars mostly south of the square/circle. Occasionally, I heard gossip about someone who was "different," but it was decades before anyone would talk about gay liberation, and closets would be for clothes rather than for coming out. Despite the era of civil rights, black and white interaction in Monmouth was slight and the Hispanic population almost nonexistent. The women's movement was understood by students only as younger teachers mentioned it in the schools, and divorce happened occasionally but was discussed in hushed tones.

A Maple City childhood

Like many a small town existing in cornfields, the inhabitants of Monmouth created their own entertainment. Little Lions League and the Motor League provided baseball, and the YMCA hosted basketball. Many of the townspeople cheered from the stands at the college games each season. Dances took place at the Farm Bureau and the YMCA, and skating parties occurred monthly at the Rainbow Roller

Rink for the elementary kids. The Rivoli Theatre scheduled only "wholesome movies," and kids could go for thirty-five cents and pay a nickel for candy. (This is where I should be humming the theme song from *Leave It to Beaver*.)

Socio-economic layers and racial divides were well defined in the 1960s, and I was familiar with them from my own hometown. Monmouth had a poorer side of town called the "South Side." Swimming was an example of the social divisions enforced in both overt and covert ways. Students from poorer families often went to Citizen's Lake to swim in the summer, while more middle-class families sent their kids to Lake Warren for swimming, boating, and camping. Kids from wealthier families swam at the more exclusive country club. After I had lived there for a while, I realized that neighborhood schools perpetuated these class issues. But despite their attending one of four neighborhood elementary schools, most of my students spent their last six years together in junior high and high school.

For someone like me who had attended a highly liberal college and strongly supported liberal social causes, this new job would be an exercise in learning to keep my mouth shut.

My mantra at that moment: "I have a job! Someone actually wants me!"

Then reality set in. Remember, this was 1968.

Obviously, the school had no computers, no calculators, no Xerox machines, and no well-developed curriculum plan. I had to figure grades by hand, using long division, and I was given a set of textbooks containing black-and-white photos and extremely small print … oh, and a key to my room. That was it.

    Looking back at that beginning, I remember vividly all that I had to learn. Technology came in the form of 16 mm projectors that took tedious practice and a lot of swearing to thread. The first time I showed multiple reels of a movie, I ended up rewinding it backwards and inside out. Two of the other teachers helped me unroll hundreds of feet of film throughout my room, trying to get it back on the reels correctly. We also had heavy, gray metal opaque projectors that I could hardly lift, which were the forerunners of overheads. To print multiple copies, we used something called a ditto machine. You wrote or typed what you wanted to copy on two-layered papers, the bottom paper having ink on it. If you forgot to take out the thin brown paper in the middle that protected the master copy on the top, you had to write it all over again. Then you tore off the master copy, clipped it onto the circular drum of the ditto machine, and cranked a handle to make multiple copies. The drum contained a breath-stopping, clear-colored vile liquid that had to be refilled through a small hole in the top of the drum. If you accidently left your master copy clipped to the machine while refilling the drum, you often ruined the copy with excess, spilled liquid. It was an evil machine, and I often cursed it, hoping it would live out its last days buried in a swamp. Of course, this probability wasn't too likely in Illinois.

    Despite this small-town atmosphere, I was always aware of world events and pop culture during my years in college and my first fall in Monmouth. Watching the local and national news on TV, I was mesmerized, because 1968 was a violent year of political assassinations, the Democratic Convention in Chicago, protesting flower children, and Vietnam. The radio was on and I listened to the latest songs while I graded papers. The soundtrack in my head was from *Hair*, the Stones, Smokey Robinson, CCR, the Supremes, Cream, Simon and Garfunkel, Grace Slick and the Jefferson Airplane, Steppenwolf, and Neil Young.

In fact, I would often hum "Jumpin' Jack Flash" on my way to school. This running sound track was a far cry from the theme song of *Leave It to Beaver*. And that route to school was only about a block.

On Broadway sat huge old mansions that were built during the earlier days of the town. My husband and I first lived in an apartment in one of those old mansions. Built by the McCullough family and later known as the John Allen house, the huge home had been divided into five apartments, and we had the entire first floor. My husband would drive our car to his teaching job in the Warren district, and I could simply walk the tree-lined block to school.

The John Allen house where we first lived.

During those years when I taught at Monmouth High School, the student population would fluctuate between five hundred and seven hundred. Previous to my grand entry into town as a real teacher, the school district had broken into two totally separate districts. Rural districts surrounded the city school where I taught. One, called Warren, was begun by disgruntled taxpayers and farmers who formed their own district because they wanted more say in how their tax money was spent, and they took their tax money from farm acreages with them. This happened just prior to my glorious arrival, so I would be teaching mainly "city" kids—but small-town city kids.

Over the course of my career, I saw many changes to both the town and the school district. In 1974, an arsonist burned an entire block of the downtown in the middle of the night, causing a six-alarm response, and I would peacefully sleep through it all, only two blocks away. That alone should indicate how exhausting teaching could be. A new highway appeared between Monmouth and Galesburg, updating the two-lane, curvy connection between the two towns.

Despite these updates, people and stores eventually left the town, and it slid economically downward, while the college continued to grow after the '70s and to help Monmouth survive. The school district switched from neighborhood elementary schools to attendance centers in order to save money, and eventually the Monmouth schools consolidated with a smaller district to the south in Roseville, ending forever the history of Monmouth High School, except in its graduates' memories.

No longer would their colors be maroon and gold, and their team names would switch from Zippers to Titans. This economically necessary consolidation would happen after I retired in 2002. The town changed and so did I. Over those many years my edges were smoothed and my sometimes abrasive opinions learned a new word: tact.

The first year I taught in the high school, my pay was $4,800 gross—but it was my first real job! By the time the district removed union dues, pension, and taxes, I didn't have much left. But I should repeat: it was my first real job!

For this princely sum, I taught five English and speech classes,

Home of the Zippers

directed a class play, helped guide a speech team, and organized a traveling debate team. It was exhausting and exhilarating because I was doing what I had wanted to do since eighth grade, when I first imagined my future career: I was a teacher.

And why? I always thought I could do something to change the world back in the 1960s when I was studying in college. Sure, it was a naïve idea, but you have to remember that I came of age when John F. Kennedy was advising me to "ask not" what my country ... well, you get the idea. I could spend my days enhancing peoples' lives in this life I was given, however short or long. I could work as a cooperating teacher with college students who wanted to teach, and I could change the world, one teacher at a time. It seemed to me that education was the key to making life better. Reading and writing—both skills I loved—could be passed on to others. Why couldn't I take something that I felt passionate about and help someone else feel the same way? The "I" is what consumed my thinking as a twenty-one-year-old. Back then, I couldn't begin to imagine the students who would come into my life and change forever both me and my thinking.

* * *

But I didn't know any of this on that 1963 visit when I attempted to find the college library. Five years later, when I drove into town on the two-lane, impossible-to-pass-farm-equipment highway, college degree in hand and teaching certificate to register, I was twenty-one, just married, and ready to tackle whatever a new teacher had to do. I was driving 60 mph behind the farm equipment—combine or cultivator?—and passing whenever I could. I was sure I had

45 mph? You're kidding!

the answers to what I needed to know about teaching five classes a day in a real high school. Passionate, fired up, amazingly young, and full of energy, I was ready!

I had no idea what was coming or how naïve I was.

Chapter Two

War and Remembrance

How does one teach during wartime? In 1968, at age twenty-two, I had all the answers and few questions. But now in 2010, at age sixty-three, I have too many questions and few answers. How do I explain the final part of the puzzle that came over dinner twenty-three years after my graduation from college? One question in particular haunts me still: Did I serve my students well by not speaking out?

When I accepted my first teaching job, I had plenty of questions to consider. An exhilarating time of great possibilities, 1968 was also a grim time of war. I was a political moderate when I left college but a solid pacifist about the Vietnam War. I argued repeatedly with my friends about the reasons for going to war, the government's spin on what was happening there, and the bogus casualty statistics—I was sure I had all the answers. But when I began teaching in a public, tax-supported high school, personal views and professional responsibility were also at war. That the small town where I taught was conservative became quite obvious when I signed a page of my contract stating that I was not a Communist and didn't plan to overthrow the government—my first hint. I had argued with myself about ethics but finally decided my teaching should reflect that conventional community.

So what stand should I adopt in my speech classes when discussing current events? While I believed I had the right to free speech, I decided on a neutral stance, encouraging students to speak out and back up their views with reasoned, civil discourse.

I rebelled in less political ways, such as allowing my students to choose psychedelic yellow paint for the classroom walls, and I joined them in peaceful painting while listening to their views on the Kent State shootings.

By the spring of 1969, I was twenty-two, sure of myself, right in my convictions, and walking the neutrality line.

Imagine psychedelic yellow wall with orange, blue, and red student profiles

A 2003 college reunion reminded me of those younger days from my college years of 1964–1968. Ahead of its time, Knox College had filmed each senior year—both ordinary and extraordinary days—and when classes returned, they could see themselves as they had been. Watching that 1968 video, I smiled as I saw my much-thinner self with long, dark hair, laughing for the camera as I stuffed tissue into chicken wire on a homecoming float. Fascinated, I focused on the screen as more ordinary days appeared. Classes were letting out and through the doors of the venerable brick-and-mortar Alumni Hall came the engineering students, all males, wearing their letter jackets and carrying impossibly heavy textbooks. At yet a different door, the education classes poured out in a stream of female students, skirt hems above their knees and hair lengths curving up from their shoulders. One or two male students swam at the rear of the flock. Then the camera switched to a sidewalk and a stream of faculty members leaving a college meeting. Wearing suits and dark, thin ties, the men walked down the sidewalk, smoking cigarettes and speaking with colleagues. Occasionally, a woman—the dean of women or a modern language professor—happened down the sidewalk in the wake of the men. It appeared that our video documented vivid social markers of a long ago time, markers that were ubiquitous then.

Now the camera focused on seniors playing in a faculty/student baseball game. I was both startled and shocked at the sight of a blond and ruggedly handsome friend, Cleave. Intelligent, athletic, and personable, he seemed to do everything effortlessly. Cleave was an award-winning athlete, a sociable frat guy, and a class officer. He moved with smooth and easy grace for such a solidly built football player and wrestler. I remembered his often telling me that I was way too serious. "Susan," he'd say, "enjoy yourself more. Life is short." Then he'd laugh and turn toward his girlfriend, Gwen. An only child from a tiny town in southern Illinois, Gwen humorously described her hometown as "a gas station, a church, and a few houses." Her smile was infectious, lighting up her entire face, and her hair was a dark, shiny brown. But it was her eyes that really defined her: a deep, soft, bottomless brown. And she was my friend.

During our senior year we both student-taught, got engaged, and set wedding dates two weeks apart in August. I had met and fallen in love with John, a blond, hazel-eyed, Spanish-teaching coach who was already working nearby at Warren School. After graduating from college, I was hired to teach high school English in Monmouth. I kept in touch with Gwen, and one might think our lives would be headed in parallel directions—well, not exactly. One distinction set us apart: Cleave went to Knox on a ROTC scholarship, believed in completing commitments, and was commissioned a second lieutenant in the army.

We all knew what that meant—the year was 1968.

Cleave and Gwen had a few months together while they waited to receive his notice to report. It came, and later he shipped out to Vietnam.

Meanwhile, my husband and I were in our small town, adjusting to our lives as married people and as teachers. During that first year, I would walk the block to my school, my heart in my stomach, wondering if I would remember how to teach after a weekend away. I would return home for lunch with a grateful heart that my memory was still working. Keeping faithful to my ethics, while I was at school I stolidly remained neutral on the war.

And time went on.

Christmas 1969: I received a card from Gwen, who said she hoped the war would end quickly and that Cleave would come home so they could start an actual life together. After all, they had shared dreams.

* * *

My second year of teaching was humming along. I walked home on my lunch hour whistling "Bridge Over Troubled Water." I can remember the date quite clearly: April 3, 1970. I climbed the stairs, grabbed the mail, and unlocked the door to our apartment. I set the stack of mail down on the kitchen table and pulled a yellow envelope—a telegram—out of the stack, tearing it open. I scanned the message written in capital letters and then read it again more carefully as my breath slowed to a standstill. It was from Gwen, informing me in that succinct, telegram way, that Cleave had been killed two days earlier in Vietnam.

I inhaled a huge, deep breath and slid into a chair. I could hear the kitchen clock ticking the seconds forward. All was totally quiet around me. Then my brain became operational. *Oh, my God! How could this happen? Why Cleave? Why Gwen? Why? For what reason? For what earthly or sane reason? This has to be a mistake! Nixon has been ordering troops home.* I reread the words again.

Loss, futility, disbelief. I took another deep breath. Just weeks ago I had taught the lines from Whittier's poem, "Snowbound." In it, he remembers his sister who died so young: "And yet, dear heart! Remembering thee, am I not richer than of old? Safe in thy immortality, what change can reach the wealth I hold?" And through my mind went a picture of Cleave, playing ball on a cloudless, blue-skied day near graduation, changeless and forever young.

My eyes filled with tears, and I tried to calm myself. It was so hard because the tears just kept coming and then I started sobbing. But I remember very clearly, even after forty years, the realization that I had to go back and teach. No calling in sick. No crying. One o'clock would come quickly. How could I get through this day? And with a deep sigh of resignation, I made a plan. Close the door to my pain. Hide it away for now. I would go back to school, teach the rest of the afternoon, and once it was over, I could come home and fall apart. That was precisely what I did.

The rest of that day is gone. I literally have not a single memory of what happened. I must have spoken with Gwen on the telephone but even now, I'm not sure what we said: I blocked it out because it was too, too painful.

Many years later, however, a door to that day—that telegram—opened once again in an unforeseen way.

* * *

On a sultry July night in 1991, the Monmouth class of 1971 invited me to their high school reunion at the American Legion, out by the highway. That evening at dinner, I was seated across from a former student, John Critser, whom I remembered well from his high school years. He had been a quiet, shy, soft-spoken teenager. I recalled that despite the crazy and irrational world we were living in back then, he always seemed so calm, so thoughtful, so deliberate.

John Critser, senior photo, 1971

Now, twenty years later, he was a successful research doctor who worked at the Indiana University School of Medicine. Perhaps I remembered his class fondly because it was the beginning of my career, and we were all so passionately young together. Now distinguished-looking, his hair starting to gray, John had matured, and his thoughtful manner had deepened. We talked about our families and spent a pleasant evening.

Later, saying my good-byes, I spoke last to John, thanking him for catching me up on his remarkable life. This had been an evening of colliding memories, many of them poignant and sweet. In that very instant he said something totally puzzling.

"You know, I probably wouldn't be doing this work if it hadn't been for our conversation."

I hesitated, mystified. "What conversation?"

"You remember," John said, "that day in your classroom." His eyes looked at me intently, waiting for recognition.

"Totally not following you. It's been twenty years. A lot of time and thousands of conversations have passed through my head since then."

"Such an amazing moment in my life—a turn of events that you don't even remember." He paused for a moment, smiled, and looked up. "Well, you should know."

My curiosity piqued, I listened as John's narrative took me back twenty-one years.

He began quietly enough, in his very precise speech, the clipped sentences of which were still familiar. "The year you taught my class—my junior year. Isn't it amazing how some times in life are so vivid and others pass by and you can hardly recollect a single detail? I was afraid my lottery number for Vietnam would be called, and I was confused. Enlist and get it over with? Go to college? Actually, I wasn't

Dr. John Critser

sure what I wanted to do with my life." He shook his head slowly. "What a perplexing time."

"I do remember that, John. Such a serious guy you were. Think of the tough decisions you had to make. You were so young. You all were."

"So true," he answered, still shaking his head. "But on the other hand, I felt 'serving my country' was right. I remember the culture had me confused and uncertain. This was a small, patriotic town. Conservatives everywhere. Even my friends felt they should volunteer. In fact, their 'right' point of view was to 'go over there and kill Commies.' I felt a lot of pressure to join that parade. Maybe they were right: my responsibility should be very clear. So why wasn't it clear to me?" He looked up at me briefly.

I smiled. "At sixteen or seventeen? And decisions are usually easier if we're making them for someone else. I can see why you were so conflicted."

Then he smiled. "Well, my dad was very direct, not 'conflicted' at all. I had spoken to him, and he felt the service was absolutely the wrong choice. College should be in my future and not barreling headlong into that ugly, dark hole that we were seeing on the news every night. I had already argued with myself constantly. Guns? Violence? Killing anyone seemed totally against what I believed. Then there were those discussions in your class about Kent State. You know, you talked about being able to back up our views in such confusing times. I wasn't sure what to do. After all, I was sixteen."

"I remember having guys who had graduated and gone to Vietnam come back and talk to my speech classes. I thought they might be against the war, but sometimes they weren't." I shook my head.

"I remember them too. But I'm thinking about a particular day, a day I decided to come in and talk my plans over with you. Your door was almost shut—made me waver. But I knocked and came in."

I stared at him, and an anxious shortness of breath began deep in my chest.

"You were sitting at your desk, and I hesitated because it looked like you'd been crying. So I asked you what was wrong, and you told me about your friend who had been killed. You'd just found out that day. You could hardly speak. In fact, you were not the teacher I'd heard cautioning reasoned judgment. Your fists were flying, and your voice was full of passion, and you spoke of what a waste the war was; that he shouldn't have died so young and for such a mindless cause. I'd never seen you so angry."

I sat utterly still. I felt like my breathing had stopped, and only John and I were sitting there. "John, I don't remember most of that day at all."

"Then I must be the keeper of your memory—*our* memory," he said and smiled once again. "I remember when I saw what effect his death had on your life, I pictured my parents. What if they received that telegram? What if it were me? Suddenly that war became very real to me. So I left your room feeling like I had a dilemma: be responsible for my own actions, or do what other people thought I should do." He paused and then softly added, "Spent months thinking about it: your sorrow, my father's reasoning, and my own instincts and values. Finally, I decided to go to college and not enlist. If I had gone to Vietnam, none of this might have happened. My wife and my children, that is. And then there's my medical research too." And now he looked directly into my eyes. "As young and naïve as I was, I too might have disappeared into that darkness. If I hadn't stopped by your room on that particular day of all days, well …"

For several days afterward I pondered John's words as I sorted clothes, ironed curtains, or put away groceries. No matter what I did I couldn't keep my mind away from his story. He had brought back a flood of memories that cascaded before my sad eyes. I walked to a bookshelf and picked up a yearbook from a long line of books—1972. Leafing through it, I came across the faculty section, and there I was, standing behind my speaker's stand in a gold knit dress with a high, round collar.

The picture was black-and-white, but I remembered that dress so clearly and the loose weave in the material that fell in soft folds from the darts at the waist. My hands were resting gently, confidently, on the edges of the slanted oak ledge, and my eyes were looking out at the class with a bemused half-smile on my face. What was I thinking, that twenty-five-year-old child? I had gone into teaching to change the lives of my students, and I

Yearbook picture, 1972

thought I could do that by teaching marketable skills, like writing, and food for their souls, like Shakespeare. Simply sitting at my desk in tears wasn't the way I'd imagined doing that. The ties that bind, even twenty years later—I realized how remarkable it was that Cleave's life—and death—had reached across a generation. The threads of a seam in my heart had split apart when Cleave died and come together again with John's words. He had given me an extraordinary gift.

Much later as I sat in a coffee shop in our little town, I thought about the photo of Cleave I had looked at last night after John called and asked about going out for coffee—Cleave would have been fifty-nine this year. John was fifty-two now. His hair had turned silver, and he looked every inch the research doctor that he was. It was 2005, and he had returned to our town to visit his mother. He had a powerful reputation in the research world, and he would be flying to China the following week to work on a collaborative project that would help make the human blood supply more plentiful and safer. Newspapers were on surrounding tables, and my eyes caught a small but curious headline, so I picked up the paper. As I waited for John to return from the counter with our coffee, I read the article that reminded me of Sandburg's poem "Grass." It said a former U.S. helicopter landing field in A Luoi, Vietnam, was now a playground for small children ... who know nothing of that war.

Chapter Three

Early Days: Chaos and Confusion
[With significant contributions by Dana Parker Woodall]

It didn't get scary until desks started crashing, books flew across the room, and blood dripped onto the tiles of my classroom. I had left my room for a few minutes to talk with one of my speech students in the hallway, and all of a sudden I heard desks screeching across the floor and a few muffled shouts. Dashing back in through the door, I was just in time to see Dana Woodall and Jim Buck facing off in the center of the room, while Jim Cook shoved wooden desks out of the way at warp speed. Buck and Woodall were staring at each other as if the rest of the room was gone.

Dana clenched his fists at his sides, kept his eyes on Jim's face, and smiled as he uttered, "Would you like to repeat that again? Louder? Let everyone hear?"

Jim Buck glanced around. "Why? Everybody knows it." Then his eyes locked on Dana's face.

The room was humid with tension, and I glanced at the other students who had backed away toward the edges, watching with anxious eyes or, in some cases, eager anticipation. I unlocked my mouth to yell

"Stop!" just as Jim threw the first punch, countered quite easily by Dana's fast reflexes.

"Geez, Buck! You'll have to do better than that!" Dana growled. "You couldn't hit the broad side of a—" and Jim swung again, as Dana grabbed his wrist and they both went down. Two desks were casualties in the chaos, and a couple of the girls screamed as the two bodies rolled closer and closer to them. Buck had blood on his face already—I think from his nose—and Dana was on top of him, continuing to taunt him. Then Jim Cook joined the brawl and got between the two, trying to get them to stop but to no avail. Several of the guys cheered them on, mainly those on Dana's side. Buck was sprawled on the floor with Woodall perched on top of him, and I could hear the "oofs" and the sounds of punches.

I pointed to Dave Ebersole and stammered, "Go … go to the …the office and get … get Mr. Woodall!"

"Oh, yeah!" Like a periscope, Dana's head suddenly rose above the arms and legs. "Yeah, Dave. Head toward shop class, go up the back stairs, and peek in on the girls' gym class on your way, as long as you're not in a hurry." At those departing instructions, Dave waved and shuffled away. Dana got off the floor, and Jim grabbed one of his legs, causing Dana to lose his balance and topple over as his other leg caught an overturned desk. Cook was either helping Dana or trying to stop both of them—hard to tell. When I located my voice again I yelled "Stop!" like they taught me in college, but no one paid any attention to me. The whole fight lasted only a couple of minutes, and I thought about getting in the middle of it, but I was afraid they might not recognize me in the heat of the action and knock me out. Unconsciousness would have been totally embarrassing…especially in a short skirt.

Then Mr. Woodall, the assistant principal, raced through the door with Larry Keener, another teacher, and they grabbed Cook and Buck as Dana took a last swing at Jim Buck. He landed a punch to Buck's left eye and I saw it immediately begin to swell. By then Keener had pushed Jim Cook out the door and had grabbed Dana.

It all stopped as quickly as it had begun, and it had only taken a couple of minutes. Gene Behnke, another teacher, had arrived from the hallway, taking Jim Cook by the arm, and all three boys were marched out of my room and up to the office. I looked around, shaking my head—but that wasn't the only thing shaking. My legs were so weak that I had to find a desk to sit down. The other students looked at me to see what I'd do. A few tried to right desks, avoiding the blood on the floor.

"Man, what a cool fight!" marveled Charlie Pullens, starting a replay of the action and arguing with Dave Thornton about who got the best punch in. It had been a nightmare, an absolute nightmare. And now, with the tension over, I wanted to throw up. As that possibility became reality, I stood up, ran across the hall to the teachers restroom, and lost my lunch in the first stall.

That was a Friday in early April, when spring-feverish, cooped-up students didn't want to be inside, despite the entertainment of a fight. On the following Sunday afternoon, I was sitting at my dining room table, pondering my options. How was I going to go back to school and deal with these students? I would hear from Mr. Woodall about his dispensation of justice to the three, probably the next morning. Maybe they wouldn't be in school—fighting was a suspension offense. I wouldn't have to face them for three days or so. Good. Let's see, that would be around Thursday of this week. By then I could figure out what to say. I began doodling each of their names on a piece of paper: Dana, Jim, Jim. Then I wrote "anxiety."

I mulled over my memories of my first teaching year. I had kept to the old cliché of not smiling until Christmas which was advice given to aspiring teachers concerning their discipline tactics. A small group of us eager twenty-somethings, just out of college, had replaced sixty-five-year-old teachers who were retiring and falling asleep at their desks—literally. We were quite a change for students who were used to their arthritic, hearing-challenged teachers. And they took to us in a big way, trying us out at every turn. My biggest fear that year—and subsequent years—was discipline. How was I going to keep in line these guys who were six-feet-plus, weighed more than double my 125-pound, no-muscled body, and said well-chosen zingers that totally threw me off balance, especially my dignity.

Typical taunts when I walked into my room after a weekend might be:

"Ah, got your hair cut this weekend, didn't you? Looks a little short [or it needs a bit more curl]."

"Saw you out at dinner Saturday night, and you were having a second drink. Something exotic with an umbrella. Should you be doing that when you're teaching school? What about that good role-model thing?"

After consecutive Mondays of hearing their version of my weekend, I did remember my sense of humor, but I spent late nights into early mornings putting together lesson plans and grading papers—and barely staying ahead. I had no time at all for living anything except school. Sheer exhaustion. And then I'd go to work, worried about whether I could control twenty-five kids in each class who were four years younger than I was and get them to focus on English or speech. I was afraid to send too many out of class because that might reflect badly on my ability to keep discipline.

And then there was Mr. Woodall, the assistant principal in charge of discipline situations and also the father of Dana Parker Woodall. He was in his mid-forties, I'd guess, dark-haired and he usually dressed rather dapperly in a plaid sport coat with pens in the pocket. I never knew quite how to take him—he had such a strange sense of humor. Sometimes I got it, but sometimes I had no clue if he was kidding me. I truly believed from his disingenuous smile to his well-polished shoes that he lived to make me worry. One time I asked him to write a reference letter for my college file, just in case I had to move on. In my mailbox I found a carbon copy of the letter that he assured me he'd mailed. It was glowing—until I got to the last line, which read "and she wears mini-skirts, drinks her whisky straight, and is the life of the faculty parties." Secure in the realization that this fake copy hadn't been mailed, I thought, "Well, two out of three isn't bad."

I sent an occasional student out of class when he or she definitely deserved it, especially the one who called me every name in the book, including a "goddamn bitch," and slammed my door so hard that I thought its glass windows would break. I had rules I tried to apply consistently, but sometimes when I added teenagers to those situations it was hard. We hadn't had many pointers in college for how to keep discipline in classes. So was it any wonder that this was an area where I was unsure of myself? I have to admit that it was often hard to keep from laughing at their outrageous comments. I had a face the students could easily read—the kind of face you'd invite to a poker game.

But two of those three students in the fight had faces that were very likely to hide all kinds of plots that could get them in trouble. I considered each of them. Jim Buck was a scrappy kid who wasn't very tall but was a challenging presence. He had dark brown hair that fell across his eyes and a look that said he might be a bit dangerous. His dark, brooding looks interested girls who were attracted to his "bad boy" image. I liked Jim, and I'd not had any run-ins with him, but I was always aware of his warily looking around and thinking about the odds.

Jim Cook was a most unlikely combatant. I was surprised he'd gotten involved, but then he was a friend of Woodall's. He was quite tall and lanky, with blond, wavy hair and a voice that spoke slowly, stopping first to consider what he was going to say. The epitome of a small-town kid, he always had a smile on his face and a lot of friends who appreciated his uncomplicated sense of humor. Too bad—he hung around with the wrong people this time.

Then there was Dana Woodall. He was the older son of the assistant principal and was also a husky and talented football player. He had brown hair that waved a bit, especially around his ears, and the beginning of sideburns that he was evidently growing out. He wore his glasses over eyes that peered around and sized up situations, and he was a shrewd observer of people. Generally he could be found near the main office, lounging around the student business area before classes. Dana always had a hilarious or clever comeback, so he could be a handful in class, especially if he were trying to put me off balance. He made me smile, and often I had a hard time not laughing at something he said. He was one of those exceptions I mentioned that made it tough to toe the hard-and-fast-rule line. He must have gotten that from his dad. He knew what was going on around school and town, but he kept his mouth shut about it—at least when he was around me. I thought we got along well, but there was one incident just before Christmas.

Near the end of the day in my speech class, a special announcement often came over the public address system. The previous December's messages included this one from Mr. Woodall:

"Good morning. The Catholic church has informed us that one of their Wise Men is missing from the outdoor manger scene. I'm sure none of our civic-minded students would be involved in such a display of sacrilegious pilfering, but if I'm wrong, please stop by my office with any information you may have about this situation"—here he paused before adding—"or any questions about the meaning of the words 'sacrilegious pilfering.'"

Immediately whispers and restless shuffling of books and papers began as students shifted into class time and quietly checked each other's knowledge of the crime. Of course they knew who had done it! Feigning a relaxed mood, I stood with my back and head against the chalkboard and watched them. The usual culprits were looking mighty innocent. I'd put my money on Dana Woodall, who had opened his textbook and was nonchalantly looking at the devastatingly interesting black-and-white photos of people giving speeches. He made no eye contact with anyone. It was time for another one of those teacher-to-Dana conversations.

I was sure he was involved. Usually his dad could walk down a hallway, put a hand on some kid's shoulder, and ask a pointed question to uncover information. He always knew which shoulder to squeeze.

I was amazed at the rumors he knew. But not this time. Word on the street was that no one was talking. So I stopped Dana the next day near the student business office. He was sitting on the countertop, totally relaxed, feet dangling, observing the noon-hour traffic.

"Wise Man? What Wise Man?"

"What do you know about this vanishing Wise Man, Dana?"

"Me? Nothing. Didn't have anything to do with that." He paused, then added, "But I did hear something about him. That he was on a search for myrrh, not easily obtainable in the Midwest, you know."

"And have you seen this Wise Man lately?"

"Well, let me think. The last time I saw him he had on a puffy stocking cap, which kind of muffled the glow from his crown—the better to stay incognito, of course. It didn't do much for his part in the miracle of the baby Jesus—kind of out of character—but other than that, nothing. I know nothing."

"Where did you hide him?"

"Hide him?" His eyes narrowed, and his face took on a skeptical look. Then he stared down the hallway briefly and countered, "Sounds a bit accusatory, wouldn't you say?"

"Next twenty-four hours. The 'Return of the Wise Man.' Otherwise, I'll have to go to the Wiseman-napper's father."

Dana frowned. "You know, you take all the fun out of things. Don't you have any sense of humor at all?" But that night the Wise Man mysteriously returned.

I always liked Dana, but he could totally take down my class with one of his rambling, humorous monologues about anything, and you never knew what he was going to say. He'd make up words like "emphasizational tools." One day in class I asked him what the difference was between an extemporaneous speech delivery and an impromptu delivery. He answered, to the delight and laughter of the class, that the first would be delivered with a bad attitude, like ex-temper-aceous, and the other would be a speech that you didn't have time to work on so you tried to fake out the teacher.

On another day I caught him in the hallway after a little set-to in class. "Dana, when Susan Twomey gets a 98 percent on a chapter quiz, you do not grab her paper, pull out a red marker, randomly check a number of correct answers as wrong, and wave it around for all to see, declaring it 98 percent wrong, with a huge, splashy, red 'F' you've written all over it."

"It was a visual aid. *A Scarlet Letter*. Didn't I hear you were teaching that in another class?"

Leaving those thoughts behind, I came back to my present dilemma. The three of them had gotten into this fight, and now they were going to be suspended and I would keep my credibility. I'd made it through two years without a fight, but it was always tough, worrying that it might happen. I thought of the old joke about the first-year teacher who was so anxious, so fearful, that she dreamed she went to school in her nightgown, having forgotten to dress that morning. What a crazy dream!

Suddenly I sat straight up in my chair, my eyes open wide. A dream? Did I possibly dream that fight happened? Could I have? It seemed so real. I'd gone past Mr. Woodall's office after school on Friday, but he wasn't there. Or had I? Was that Friday? Had this happened or not? Some of the details had already gotten hazy. Searching back through my mind, I recalled the rest of that day. I leaned over my dining room table, my face in my hands. It seemed so vivid: the fight, the blood, the screams, and someone's going to the office. But maybe not.

Then another reality hit me. What was I going to do the next day? I couldn't act like a crazy woman who didn't even know what had happened in my class. I couldn't go in and see Mr. Woodall if this had been a dream. Boy, would I hear about that one from him forever and ever. I moved some pencils across the table and looked down at the paper I'd been grading, but my concentration was gone. How would I figure out what to do? If the boys had been suspended, I'd probably not see them at school on Monday morning. Maybe I could go up to the office, nonchalantly check the attendance list after first hour, and see if they were in school. Yes! That would work. If it hadn't been a dream, Mr. Woodall would have suspended them.

* * *

Monday morning came with its usual dread, and I plodded the block to school early, book bag and papers in hand, hoping I could slip in without anyone's noticing. No such luck. As I came in through the north door and paused on the stairway landing, I could see Mr. Woodall standing in his usual spot by the main office. His demeanor reflected a "Definite"—with a capital D—morning. If you had a question, he had an answer. Sometimes you couldn't tell if it was true or made-up, but he could deliver it with charm.

His face broke into a huge grin when he saw me—I was a rookie target—and he leaned over the stairwell to look down at me. "Well, good morning, Sunshine!"

I started down the stairs, hoping to end the conversation. "Morning, Mr. Woodall."

"Keeping a good eye on those junior boys?"

I paused two steps down and looked up, thinking, *What junior boys? The fight?* "Sure. Always."

"Good. Especially that Woodall kid."

"Dana?"

"Well, sure. He can be a handful sometimes." And he smiled broadly.

"Of course." And I walked on downstairs, wondering what he meant by that. Was Dana suspended or not?

After first hour I did get a chance to go up to the main office and check the attendance list. Buck was gone and so was Cook. Hmm. But Dana was here. What was this? A cover-up? Did only two guys get suspensions? How could Mr. Woodall do that? His own son! If I were the other parents, I'd be storming the office. However, I still didn't see any suspension notices in my mailbox. *Was my dream theory possible?* Over the noon hour, I took an attendance slip to the office, and as I walked out the office door I saw Dana in his usual perch at the student business office.

He nodded and said, "Mrs. Van Kirk."

"Hi, Dana. How's it going?" He scrutinized my face. The last time he saw me might have been during his hasty exit through my door to his father's office.

"Oh, let's see. It's Monday morning. I worked at the IV 'til almost 1:00 last night. I'm here. I'm awake. Pretty much gotten past the end of the week's baseball loss, and we have another game this Thursday." He paused and looked around. "Astoundingly average, I'd say!"

"Any idea where Buck and Cook are today?"

"Naw. Most weeks I'm only on duty watching them on Tuesdays and Thursdays. Any reason why I should?"

"Just wondered. They don't seem to be here according to the attendance list."

"They're probably ..." He scratched his cheek for a moment, and I noticed deep bruising on his right hand knuckles. That was it! I knew it! He'd been in that fight on Friday after all. So why was he at school today while the other two weren't?

"Dana, let me see your hands." I grabbed his hands and held them out, examining them.

"You really think this is right? I mean, you being married, a teacher, and all? I mean, this isn't at all unpleasant, but mightn't some of those in the educational structure of things here maybe view this sort of public display of affection as ..." He paused, then added, "Improprietious?"

Ignoring him, I demanded, "How did you get all those bruises?"

His face took on the same disingenuous look as Woodall Senior. "Remember the end of the week? Baseball game? Hit by an errant pitch?"

Was that the truth? It was the same hand he'd used on Jim Buck last Friday. Maybe.

"Should you be here today?"

He raised an eyebrow and laughed. "Well, I appreciate your concern that I was pretty beaten up at the game, but of course I'm here today! A few bruises couldn't keep me home."

I wasn't going to get anything out of him. Time to go to class. Abruptly, I said, "All right. I'll see you downstairs."

As I walked down to my room, I thought, *I should simply ask him. Just come right out and ask if he was in a fight in my class on Friday.* What else could I do? And where were Buck and Cook? I fumed all the way down to my room. He was just like his father—a regular tag team, they were—and you could never get a straight answer out of either of them.

Finally, just before my last class, I stood out in the hallway, watching teenagers go in my door. After a while, I walked in and went to my desk to pick up my plans; other students arrived and sat down. I pulled out an attendance sheet and stood behind the speaker's stand, ready to begin the hour. The last to arrive was Dana. What was I to make of this? Dana but no Jims.

"We're going to do some impromptu speaking today to see if you can think on your feet and to work on giving yourselves more confidence. So first we'll draw a number for the speech order."

I walked around the room, holding a box of paper slips with a number on each. Several students pulled out their numbers and either groaned or applauded. When I reached Dana, I held up the box and his bruised hand pulled out a paper slip with the number one on it.

"Oh, great! This thing had to be rigged. Okay, I can take a joke." Then his face changed as he looked around. "Wait a minute. Thanks! This way I won't have time to get nervous. I'm through, and I can enjoy the rest of you suckers' acts."

After passing out numbers, I went around with slips of paper with topics listed on them. Each student chose two slips and decided which topic to use. Dana, of course, did his decision-making out loud.

"So I have to either speak on how I'd raise my children or elaborate on what species of tree I would be if it were up to me. Honestly, being totally uninformed on each of these choices, let's see ... my sheltered upbringing as opposed to how I'd raise my kids, when and if that dilemma were ever to occur, or arborally defining myself. Well, trees it is. Scientifically, trees have been here way longer than we humans, so I'd assume that, despite never having studied trees, I should fare much better with elaborating on what I would choose to be my deciduous lifestyle. Philosophically, mind you, if I were a tree and for some reason fell and there was no one in the forest to hear, would I make any noise?"

"Dana, I can't imagine your not making noise in any situation. Stop pontificating and go up and give the speech from the speaker's stand."

So he headed up to the front, looked around the room, and launched into one of his characteristic, rambling monologues.

"Trees have always fascinated me ..." he began, and for several minutes he intricately intertwined fact and total fiction about trees, leaves, and forests. I hadn't indicated a maximum time for these talks, so he kept rambling, and I wondered where he might be going with this and, more important, for how long. Just as I was wondering about Dana's shut-off switch, I saw the door quietly open next to him, and Jim Cook and Jim Buck wandered in. They were holding admit slips that were the color of excused admits because of college visits. Jim Buck made a sweeping bow and Dana, his rhythm broken, greeted them with "Gentlemen, as long as you've dropped by, might I use you as gen-u-wine, first-rate visual aids in my talk here?"

Pulling Cook to his left, Dana said, "Trees vary quite a bunch, like my example here—a tall, majestic redwood, straight and strong." Then placing Buck on his right, he continued, "While the oak here is a bit smaller and always shady. I believe I'd be a sycamore tree, with widespread limbs and gigantic, easy-to-rake leaves. So, in conclusion, as long as we've 'breached' the topic of leaves, it would only be fitting that the three of us do." And in a sideways shuffle, arm in arm, with no synchronization whatsoever, they took a vaudeville-like stage exit, with Dana exclaiming, "We leaves!" And they exited, stage right.

The class erupted with laughter and the three reentered, bowing as their audience applauded. Once again, Dana had taken over, but at this point, I did not even care. No one noticed the teacher in the back who, checking out Jim Buck's face for signs of combat, breathed a sigh of relief that she would still have her job and had protected her reputation for sane thinking with the assistant principal.

Looking back at that day, as a confident veteran teacher, I remember the dreadful fear I experienced when I first taught real students—not imaginary, theoretical college classes. The cooperating teacher parachute—someone to pick me up when I failed—was no longer available, and it took several years to get the discipline right. I learned to draw a tight line between what I would and wouldn't tolerate, and I got much better at tempering that with a sense of humor and a demand for the same respect I showed my students—respect, not friendship. In all the years I taught, I had only one almost-fight. Several sophomore football players in my class who would be playing in the state football finals the following week, held their black star player back when another student, who was white, muttered a racial epithet under his breath. I didn't have to do a thing because they knew suspension was not an option here.

Dana went on to live a most extraordinary life and to this day, I'm sure he has a remembered fondness for deciduous trees.

Chapter Four

"Hi! I'm Barb. I Sneeze."

I stare straight ahead at the faucet in the kitchen sink; then at the curtains over the sink, the light over the curtains. Now down to the glasses balanced precariously on the metal border strip between the sink and the counter. I take another breath.

"Okay, let's do this," my mother says in my ear, her voice soft but definite. I'm sitting on her lap, her arms enfolding me.

"No, wait a minute. Just let me get one more breath." I look around and remind myself to think. I'll be ready in a minute. "I promise. Just one more look, Mommy."

My mother glances at my father. He backs away from me for the fourth or fifth time, hesitant, and pauses for a moment. In that space I notice the faucet, the curtains, the glasses, and the oblong, brown box packed with tiny bottles on the counter. Turn my head. Look down. The square, green-gray tiles in the floor my parents laid out and glued one by one. The bottom of the chair legs touching the floor. My mother's slim ankles and then the front of her legs and then the edge of her sky-blue pedal-pushers. How much longer?

"Suzy, we have to get this over with," my father says. His hazel-blue eyes look into mine, then into my mother's. He moves toward me awkwardly, apologetically.

"Okay," I say in a tiny voice, my lower lip trembling just a little.

My mother's hands tighten. I feel my body stiffen. My father comes forward, and I can't look at his hands. I close my eyes and hold my breath, and there's a sudden prick in my arm—and then it's over, and it hurts, and I'm crying.

My father picks up my impossibly thin five-year-old body, holds me in his arms, and tells me he's sorry and that it hurt him to do this. Eventually, my sobs subside to sniffles, and I realize it's all over for another week.

In 1951, when I was five, my parents made a remarkable decision. They loaded my nine-year-old brother and me in our dark green 1946 Buick and drove 712 miles from our home to the Balyeat Hay Fever and Asthma Clinic in Oklahoma City. Remarkable, because my father worked three jobs to pay the bills, and although we lived in our own house, his income for that year was only $4800. As he later said in his matter-of-fact way, "Your mother and I were young then, just thirty-one, and we had more courage. You see, my dear, we simply had no choice." During that one-week, no-other-choice-consultation, my father was taught to give me the hurtful, hated allergy shots that we would repeat once a week—two shots, every Sunday night, for years on end.

Mainly through my parent's sacrifice and love, I survived those early years, but I never would outgrow the allergies and their accompanying asthma. They were often on my mind throughout college, and when I began teaching high school English, the pollen-filled autumns and springs were hard on my breathing in the non-air-conditioned Midwest buildings in which I studied or worked. I could never have imagined that those anguished Sunday nights with my parents, so vividly imprinted on my childhood memory, would become part of the tapestry of my teaching, until a resolute teenager named Barb Stansell sneezed her way into my life.

*   *   *

On a hot, leaf-burning day toward the end of September 1969, I settled in to begin informative speeches in my fourth-hour speech class. An air of expectancy, an anticipation that something exceptional was about to happen, hung over the room. Looking up, I noticed furtive glances in the direction of the towering blonde girl in the third seat of the middle row: Barb Stansell. She shuffled well-worn note cards in her hands and glanced over them one last time, her lips moving silently. Without so much as a glimpse at my list of speakers, I said clearly and without hesitation, "Okay, Barb, let's start with you."

I realized that everything would depend on the first thirty seconds.

Karen Rousey and Bonnie West sat back in their seats feigning relaxation, but I was aware of Karen's drumming her fingers on the edge of her desk; Bonnie just looked straight ahead. Twenty-four students were in the audience, and I glanced at each of them. Chuck straightened some papers; Albie leaned back and watched Barb—she slid sideways and pushed out of her desk to stand up—and Mary closed a book she was reading. The rustling of paper, the uncommon stillness, a quiet so profound I could hear the wall clock ticking—all these marked Barb's rising from her seat and walking solemnly, hands folded, to the speaker's stand. She was like, I thought, Anne Boleyn on her way to the executioner's platform.

The speaker's stand—a massive oak bulwark—offered some respite from the terror of standing alone at the front of the class. Now Barb set her note cards on its slanted wooden shelf. I could see that her hands were shaking only slightly. I glanced at her imposing five-foot-ten frame, her squared shoulders, and the top of her blonde head as she leaned over and looked down at her notes. Her long wavy hair curled around her neck, and she pushed back either side of the blond layers and secured them behind her ears. Then she glanced at her note cards. Her hand reached up momentarily and she self-consciously touched the top button on her blouse. She cleared her throat but stood silently for five more beats. Then, taking a deep breath, she spoke quietly, masking any agitation she felt but hardly glancing up from her notes. Telltale pink blotches began to appear on her skin, just below her chin and above the top button of her blouse. As she completed her first sentence, she paused, but the pinkness continued to creep slowly upward. Karen glanced at Bonnie, and Chuck's hand tightened its grasp on the edge of his desk. Judy flicked several page corners of *The Scarlet Letter* that rested on the left side of her desk top. Albie sat back and calmly chewed gum. I glanced at the impossibly slow hand of my stopwatch as it hit the ten-second mark.

The previous year—my first year of teaching—the world was falling apart in Southeast Asia, but here in west central Illinois, I fought a more minor war. My students, unbeknownst to me, engaged in devious schemes to break in the new teacher. By the time I met Barb, her contemporaries had tried an assortment of underhanded and often entertaining campaigns to either make my life miserable or expose my naiveté.

My rookie classroom was in the basement of an old brick high school with the word "lunchroom" over the door. It had evidently served this purpose in the past, but with enrollment climbing, the tiny, stark room, with its pinkish-gray walls and hard tile floors, had been pressed into service—and as a first-year teacher, I often wondered if I were going to be the lunch. Besides the usual bookshelves, blackboards, and old-fashioned wooden desks that inhabited the room, the lights hung a foot below the ceiling, casting a feeble glow on desktops that had carved messages from long-ago occupants.

Tall wooden windows graced the entire north wall—they could be closed only by using a long pole with a hook at the end. Because the bottom frames rested right at ground level, stray dogs and cats joined our class from time to time and always were a welcome distraction to the students. In addition to encouraging these animal forays, the seniors had tried to convince me that it was customary on Fridays for one of them to leave class by way of these windows, slink along the base of the building near the principal's office—but well underneath his radar—and hoof it the two blocks to the Pastry Palace, where he would buy doughnuts for the whole class.

I didn't buy that one—the glazed doughnuts or the deep-fried story.

Then there was what I can refer to only as the "Poe Incident." I was sitting on a stool in front of the class, my American literature text open on my lap, reading aloud a passage from Edgar Allan Poe's "The Fall of the House of Usher." We were down in the Usher dungeon, where it was dark, decaying, and depressing, heading for Madeline's coffin, anticipating that she had been buried alive. Footsteps, door hinges creaking, flickering torches, and the creepiness of underground passages filled the last sentence. Everyone's eyes were glued to their textbooks. All of a sudden, Paul Wheeler interrupted me with grave intensity as he rose from his seat.

"Mrs. Van Kirk!" My head and shoulders jerked, and I looked up. "Stop reading, but keep totally still and don't move! Your life depends on it!"

Amused and wondering what the joke was this time, I did as he suggested. Quietly, he crept up right in front of me, eyes intently focused. He took my open book, raised it above my face, and slammed it shut just inches above my head. The room exploded in hysterical laughter. He grinned, and I drew myself up with my most teacher-like authority and started to tell him to head for the principal's office. That was when he opened the book and showed me the remains of a huge spider that had been patiently inching its way down a thread just above my face but which now was entombed forever in Poe's prose. He turned and bowed to wild applause and whistles.

All right, so that one I believed.

With those experiences fresh in my mind, was it any wonder that the following year, after I assigned the first speech, I didn't believe Barb Stansell's two friends, Bonnie West and Karen Rousey, when they stopped by my room after school to tell me that Barb couldn't give a speech.

"What do you mean, she can't give a speech?"

Karen sucked in a deep breath, glanced at Bonnie, and said in an ominous tone, "We mean you'll be incredibly sorry if you have her do this. Seriously."

I decided to humor them. I smiled. "How can you take a speech class and not give speeches?"

"Well," Bonnie chimed in, "she's taking the class precisely because it *is* a speech class. We figured you might as well know. Everyone else does. You see, she sneezes."

I cocked my head to one side. "Sneezes?" I studied them. They seemed sincere, but then I had thought that before to my dismay.

"Yes," Bonnie said, brightening at the thought that she now totally commanded my attention. "Sometimes a hundred times."

"What? You have to be kidding." I laughed. "You really think I'm gonna buy that?" They stood there totally adamant, both frowning at my humor. I stopped laughing. I would get to the bottom of this, so I played along. "Oh, right. And how might you know that? Have you counted her sneezes?"

Karen smiled at Bonnie, and with a decidedly ironic tone, she added, "What do you think, Bonnie? Did we count her sneezing anytime in the last six years?"

"Don't you know it! In fact, the whole class has counted her sneezes. We even took bets on speaking assignments—you know, how many times teachers would give her one before they gave up and let her do something else."

A dangerous trio: Barb, Bonnie, and Karen in 1973

Karen put her hands on her hips and rolled her eyes. "I made absolutely nothing because her teachers never get past speech one."

"Well, I'll tell you what, girls. I think I'll go ahead and have Barb speak and see how it goes. Maybe she'll be miraculously cured by tomorrow." I raised one eyebrow and smiled. "I do believe in miracles, you know."

They looked at each other with grim resignation. Karen pointed her index finger at me as they edged away. "Don't say we didn't warn you."

High drama, indeed!

The next day I began autobiographical speeches, which went reasonably well. I picked students at random, and they had to talk for only three minutes. Barb Chamberlin had just finished hers, and everyone clapped politely as she sat down.

"Barb Stansell, you're on!"

Barb picked up her notes and walked slowly to the front of the room. I just knew the slow, deliberate walk was a teaser, part of the plot. As I glanced up at Bonnie and Karen, they both turned toward me and slowly shook their heads in unison. *Right!* I thought. I picked up my critique sheets, straightened them, and then readied my pen. By now, Barb was behind the speaker's stand. She hesitated, I nodded and smiled, and she took a deep breath. Her first sentence came out slowly but reasonably well. *I was so right about this one!* By the time she reached her fourth sentence, however, she hesitated, turned her head to the side, and sneezed.

Hmm, I thought. *You'll have to do better than that.*

"I'm sorry, I—" And another sneeze came tumbling out. Karen and Bonnie shook their heads and, as I watched, the sneezes multiplied like the brooms and buckets in the old Disney movie, "Fantasia." Over and over she sneezed until I walked up to the front of the room and said, "It's okay. Stop the speech. Let's get your sneezes stopped. We'll talk later." Gratefully, she nodded and sneezed a couple more times. Both of us were shaken. We walked back to our desks and sat down. Bonnie and Karen stared knowingly at me as if to say, "Stupid woman! You should have listened to us."

Albie Huff, sitting in the front row, offered, "Now *I* would like to critique that unique and highly unusual speech."

"Thanks for the offer, Albie. I think I'll pass on your comments this time."

"But I—"

"Enough!" Someone snickered, and the room erupted in noise and talking. Albie turned around for the moment, laughing, and murmured something to Mary. I could feel my heart pounding. What had just happened? The room was a mass of noise and talking, so I called the next girl, Judy Bersted, to give her speech.

It was a wonder I could concentrate on anything she said. I divided my attention between watching Barb and listening to Judy. Barb appeared to be settling down, and her skin returned to its normal, pale tone. As time went by, she seemed to relax, but her head was down and her shoulders rounded. I caught her as the bell rang and told her I would get back to her tomorrow about her speech. As I watched, Bonnie and Karen flanked Barb on either side and headed out the door, like tackles guarding a wide receiver.

I had little time to think about the "Barb problem" until early afternoon. That was my first break, when I'd have time to do some investigating. I figured the counseling office was the place to start. Catherine Hamilton, the girl's counselor, was a tall, regal woman—stylish in her clothing, resolute in her opinions, clear in her speech. She had given me some help on earlier occasions when I had asked about particular students.

I sat down in the chair opposite her imposing desk and thought about the best way to start.

"Barb Stansell," I said.

"Ah, yes. A lovely girl." She smiled. "What would you like to know about her?"

"Can you tell me a little bit about her background?" I tapped my pencil on my leg, thinking about how best to describe Barb's unusual behavior.

Mrs. Hamilton got up, turned toward a filing cabinet, opened the middle drawer marked "sophomores," thumbed through several tabs, and pulled out a folder. She sat back down, opened it, and began leafing through the papers.

"Her background … well, let's see. Her father's a lawyer. Mom stays at home and takes care of the kids. There are three. Barb has an older sister—utterly amazing girl—who just graduated and is now in college. She's very accomplished, ambitious, graduated at the top of her class here. Then there's a younger brother. Don't know much about him yet."

"So Barb is in the middle, following the amazing sister."

"Yes. Does well in her academics but seems pretty quiet. She's mainly involved in the music program." Her face scrunched up as she tried to recall. "Plays … the flute, maybe? Oh, I can't remember. Anyway, that's pretty much what I know about her."

"I have her in a speech class." I paused, looking up. *Not* in my English class." Was it my imagination, or did a momentary flicker of concern cross her face?

"Oh."

"She seems to have an unusual problem. I'm not sure what to do about it, and I thought maybe you could give me some advice. You know," I said, shaking my head, "nothing I learned in college helps me with this one. I'm not sure what to do—it has me really puzzled."

She closed the folder, put her hands on top of it, looked up at me, and said, "Oh, you mean the sneezing problem."

"You know about this?"

"Well, sure. Actually, a lot of people know about this. When I was scheduling her for this fall, the other speech teacher thought you might be able to handle it better than she could, so I put her in your class. You're young. You have lots of good ideas. I figured you could help her with this thing."

I rubbed the back of my neck and crossed one leg over the other, shifting my weight in the chair. "Does everyone know about this? Hasn't anybody been able to help her with it? And how did she get this far when she has this problem?"

"Well …" Catherine's voice dropped a bit, as if she were thinking about how much to say. "Sue, I've gotta tell ya, I'm not sure when all this started. I've heard it was somewhere back in the lower grades. I don't know much more than that. I think her other teachers just passed her on—gave her a pass on giving talks. It was just easier than trying to deal with it. Can't blame 'em. I wouldn't have a clue where to start either."

"I can't give her a pass. Think about how this cripples her. She'll never be able to do anything that involves talking in front of groups. I was hoping you could give me some idea of where to start."

"Not … a … clue."

"All right." I got up slowly, grabbing my purse from the floor and feeling impossibly alone. "I'll do some thinking about this. Maybe … maybe I can come up with something."

"Good luck. If there's anything I can do to help, just let me know."

I walked home from school that day thinking I had to come up with a plan. But what? I wondered what Barb thought of it herself. I decided to find out the answer to this question by meeting with her. I would get her away from school and talk to her on neutral ground.

The next day Barb and I walked the block to my apartment. Once there, I gestured for her to sit on the sofa in my living room, got her a soda, and plopped down in a chair across from her. After some preliminary chitchat, I moved to the main issue.

"So, tell me a little bit about this sneezing and your family. What do they think of it?"

She looked straight at me and said, "Well, they haven't a clue. I mean, you know, they're baffled about all this—the cause of it, that is.

We don't really talk about it. It seems to happen when I'm the center of attention. At first, they encouraged me to try new things, but always it ended with the predictable result—sneezing. They've kind of given up, I think. Most people have—given up, that is. It's just such an odd situation."

"I see. And how about your friends? I notice that Bonnie and Karen are definitely concerned about you."

"Yeah. It's not as if anyone can help. I do everything I can to stay out of the limelight. Even the instrument I play in the band keeps me in the middle, not on the edges. That could be scary. Can you imagine in the middle of a concert? I could probably sneeze to the beat of whatever we were playing," she said. She laughed softly but I noticed a slight edge to her voice.

"Would it bother you to talk about when it began?"

"You mean the first time? No, not at all. I actually know exactly when it began." She took a long swig of her drink. "Fourth grade. Scary teacher. When I think back to that now, maybe she just didn't have any patience. You know, she was an older woman, probably about to retire. On the day the sneezing started, I'd torn a page in my reading book. It was just an accident and I was afraid she'd find out. That would give all the kids a laugh, you know, when she scolded me in front of everyone. And she would have. It didn't help that the class was filled with friends and kids that had been together since the early grades. You know, we knew each other well and had the same history, same jokes and stories and we giggled a lot. Unfortunately, I was kind of a class clown in that respect."

"So now it wasn't so funny? Worrying about the book page?"

"Exactly. I was really anxious. I don't remember clearly how it started, but at some point that day I sneezed. The teacher had been giving some directions, and she became angry, because I was laughing along with everyone else, not realizing how mad she was. Everyone else was giggling, and then she walked right back to my desk, and everyone hushed, waiting to see what would happen. It was the worst. She singled me out and said I had no respect and was making fun of her. And ..."

I could see her eyes getting shiny and her voice catching a bit so I jumped in. "You realized it wasn't so funny?"

"Right. I could feel myself getting really scared about what she was going to do to me. Everyone stopped laughing or talking, and it was quiet. And I mean deadly quiet. And then, to my horror, she leaned over, grabbed my arm, and told me she was going to take me to the office because I was a disrespectful, nasty little girl—or some words to that effect." I waited as Barb paused, then said, "I was so ashamed, so humiliated. My mom had to come to the school, pick me up, and take me home for the rest of the day."

"I can't imagine how horrible that must have felt."

"I was so scared and embarrassed. I guess I was feeling guilty that I could have helped that somehow. You know, not sneezed. Had I done it on purpose? I was always the one who might have a great laugh at a joke or giggle at a story, but I didn't get in trouble. And why I sneeze now, after all this time—well, actually through all these years, I don't understand. It makes no sense." She took a long breath. "I'm really tired of this."

I searched my mind for something positive to say. "You certainly have some good friends. They seem to look out for you and try to keep you out of these situations."

Barb smiled. "Oh, yeah. They've been with me all along, and they know about the sneezing. But now ... well, it screws everything up!" She stopped and thought for a moment. I waited. "It wasn't so bad at first. Teachers knew. So I'd get out of stuff, and my friends would support me. I might as well introduce myself each year by saying, 'Hi. I'm Barb. I sneeze.' It seemed like one time, just one time they'd have me get up and speak with the usual results and that finished that. But I'm getting tired of being different and ... well ... of feeling like I'm a cripple because I can't do what everyone else can do!"

"So after all this time—what? Six years?—it's beginning to get very old, I'd imagine."

"You're telling me. And there are things now I wanna do—one especially."

"And that is …?"

"Michigan. Every year my family goes up there in the summer. We have a cabin on a lake. And Karen—you know, Karen Rousey—is going to go with me. My parents said we could stay a little longer up there together, and everyone else would go home, but if we do, I'd have to have a responsible job, like life-guarding, which I really wanna do." Her voice waivered and went into resigned mode. "But last summer I tried to take a class and—of course—in the middle of it, when I had to do something while everyone watched, I started sneezing. And I'm terrified to retake it. Absolutely terrified. I know it'll happen again."

So now I knew the reason for the speech class. Finally her sneezing had become a liability instead of an asset.

"I'm determined, Mrs. Van Kirk, to do something to make this stop. So what do I do?"

Should I tell her I didn't know what to do? This was not covered in my college educational psychology book. Nevertheless, I squared my shoulders and took a stab at my best positive answer. "We're going to solve this problem—together. You've really given me a lot of clues about the situation, so I just need some time to think about it and put the pieces of the puzzle together. We'll figure out something."

"Great! I knew you could help!" She looked at me so confidently that I tried to put my most convincing look on my face.

"Okay. Why don't you give me a day or two to think about it and see what I can come up with." And with that, I began the process of "figuring it out."

Figuring it out? I had no idea where to start. That evening I thought long and hard about "the sneezer." I was determined to find a way. It seemed like a stimulus-response action. Whenever she was the center of attention, the response was to sneeze, somehow connected to her shame and humiliation. What was I—an amateur psychologist?

I thought about resources to help me: the guidance counselor, older colleagues. My own experiences seemed to be of little use. I wondered, Why me? Barb had crossed the paths of multiple teachers but for some reason she chose to confront this with me. Perhaps it was just a matter of timing. I came along when Barb had reached an age where she had opportunities she couldn't take. Besides feeling empathy for her, I was twenty-three, an age when I felt no problem was too hard to solve. I would sleep on this one, because I had often experienced situations where "sleeping on it" let my subconscious chew away at whatever was bothering me.

Allergy shots—the next morning I woke up thinking about allergy shots, and suddenly I came upon a plan for Barb that might do the trick: desensitization. Just as my shots had made me less sensitive to allergens, maybe multiple exposures to being the center of attention could desensitize Barb to the response of repeatedly sneezing. It was worth a try.

"I think you should put together a short speech," I told her the next day after class.

"Why? I'll just start sneezing again."

"I have a plan. Trust me."

And she did.

She put together a speech about her church youth group's trip to Marcy Newberry Center in Lawndale, Illinois. It wasn't very long—only a few minutes—but I felt it would work. A few days later, I asked her to come in after school.

"You're going to give the speech, using your notes, and not look up at all. Just read the whole thing. Don't look up. Pretend you're just reading to yourself."

"Okay," she said, puzzled. "And where will you be?"

"I'll be in the back at my desk grading papers. I won't look at you at all. In fact, I'll ignore you."

She laughed. "This is the craziest experiment I've ever seen."

"Just wait. You'll see. There's a method to my madness."

So she read the entire speech and not a sneeze came out of her. She did this each day for a week and I always praised her. We were ready for the next step.

"Now, I want you to give the speech for me, but you can look up as much as you want. I'll look up, too, but just a little. If things go okay, I'll look up more as the week goes by."

This step worked also, but I have to say we were both getting really tired of this friggin' trip to Lawndale. And then it was on to friends. Each noon hour, one of Barb's friends would come in and listen. Eventually we worked up to three or four friends. If she sneezed, which she occasionally did, we dropped back to one friend. It worked.

One day she asked, "So, things seem to be working. When can I give it for the class?"

She wanted to push harder and try more, and I had a tough time getting her to see that we had to take it slowly. What I didn't tell her was that I was afraid of a setback if she started sneezing again. One bad time and we would be back to square one.

On to the next step.

The following day I sent Barb to the library. While she was out of the room, I announced to the class that tomorrow, Barb would give a speech for them, but they were to do homework and not look up at her. Everyone looked around at each other and at me. No one said anything, but they looked curious—they wanted Barb to do something she'd never done before. Albie raised his hand and gave me his usual "Gee, there's something I'm not sure of" look that generally signaled a remark that would entertain the class. But this time he just said, "Do you want me to sit outside just in case I can't keep control of myself?" He glanced around; smiling faces were waiting for my answer.

"I think, Albie, that on this occasion, you can work very hard at self-control."

"Oh." He paused for a moment and then said, "All right. I'll practice that before I come in tomorrow."

"Good. It would mean a lot to Barb, and it would save the principal having to keep your chair free outside his office."

What followed were several days when Barb was able to give her speech to the class without looking at her audience.

And so we finally came to the day when she gave a new speech, one she had made up and would give while looking up. She was thirty seconds into the speech. All through the classroom, people were holding their breath, including me. Bonnie, Karen, and her friends, who had seen Barb fail so many times, were looking straight at the front, not daring to turn toward each other. As soon as Barb said her last sentence she paused, looked up, broke into a smile, and held her hands up triumphantly. Everyone jumped out of their seats and congratulated her. The noise alone could have brought the principal.

The rest of the world kept turning on its axis. All over our small town people went about their business, the clock routinely clicked its way toward the hour, and the halls outside my room quietly awaited students who would emerge from classroom doors. But in room ten of Monmouth High School, a unique, unimaginable, life-altering, and remarkable event had occurred. A life had changed forever.

After that day, Barb took off as if the starting gate to a new life had opened. She wanted to try out for the class play, which I directed, but I talked her into being the stage manager. I wasn't brave enough; I didn't have her courage. That summer, however, she became the lifeguard she had wanted to be in Michigan—after that, no closed gates could hold her back. The following winter, she played the part of Nancy in the high school production of the musical *Oliver!*—and she sang solos on stage.

Barb's education did not end with high school. She later earned her PhD in psychology and now works for a private corporation—she flies to various cities all over the world to help powerful CEOs learn to communicate with their employees by using effective public speaking skills. And what approach does she use? She begins by telling them, with an utterly convincing smile, that "overcoming a fear can be life-altering."

Chapter Five

A Winter Tale

"I stopped in to see if you might have some of his English papers. If you do, I'm wondering if I could have them; that is … well, if you don't need them anymore." The man hesitated, waiting, and glanced over my shoulder at the gray, cloudless sky. Outside the windows of my high school classroom, the bleak light of a February afternoon was fading to dusk. I had been grading papers when he appeared in my doorway.

"No, I'm afraid I don't. I wish I did but I'm pretty sure I don't." I shook my head briefly and put my hands in my pockets.

His hands quietly fingered the brim of the hat he held, and he turned the hat around and around in front of his stomach. He was a middle-aged man, with a solid, athletic build and far taller than my five-foot-four frame. I had watched him referee football games, where he dashed down the field with the players, always in sync with their movements, never behind. But now he leaned forward with his shoulders slightly stooped, looking much older than I remembered him. *He's tired*, I thought. *No wonder.*

"Well," he whispered, "all right." He turned to leave and inched a few steps toward my classroom door. Then he hesitated, as if he'd forgotten something, and walked back to me. "If you should come across some as you're organizing your room and your papers, would you give me a call? You know, sometimes the wife cleans the house ..." He paused while he gathered his thoughts. "And finds things in closets that she thought she'd thrown out." His voice faltered briefly, and then steadying himself, he added, "I'd appreciate it."

In my gentlest voice, I assured him, "If I find anything I'll save it for you. But usually I give assignments back. He'd probably have had any papers that he wrote." My eyes rested momentarily on a black wooden cabinet near the doorway. Briefly, the possibility that it contained several stacks of saved papers flitted through my head. Sometimes I dropped them in that deep cabinet I had dubbed "the black hole."

He pulled his shoulders back as if to indicate he'd tried. "I surely appreciate it. You know, I'd like to read them ... over again."

"Absolutely. I'll call if I find any, Mr. Petersen. I promise." I felt sure that I didn't have what he wanted, but it seemed like the right thing to say.

"Thanks." He blinked his eyes, closed them briefly, and then was out the door, pulling it shut as softly as he had spoken.

I walked slowly to the back of my room, glancing out the window at the first signs of the weather shifting into a windy March. It had been a cold, lingering winter, both outside the building and inside me. Sitting down at my desk, I picked up my pen and glimpsed the paper on top of the stack: "Why Jay Gatsby Is a Tragic Figure." I let my breath out with a sigh and stared out the window once again, trying to delay the inevitable thoughts. I sat back in my hard wooden desk chair, laid down my pen, and rubbed my chin. It had been months, but now I felt the familiar sadness creeping up on me, ambushing me in the quiet.

Four years earlier I was considering how to spark my American lit students' interest in *Spoon River Anthology*. I was in my second year of teaching high school English in the winter of 1970. *Juniors in high school believe they will live forever*, I thought. So how would I teach them this book that discussed the thin line between life and death? Edgar Lee Masters had written his *Anthology* in 1915, composing 244 poems written as epitaphs. Each deceased person spoke of his life and challenged the reader to form judgments about that life of regret, fulfillment, or so many other human emotions. The poems gave an interesting picture of small-town life, its opinions, economics, social layers, and relationships. I loved this book. The minute my students saw it I would hear the usual outcry about wasting time on poetry. So I wrote my lesson around multiple approaches. First, the small-town scandal approach. After all, Masters had revealed scores of closeted skeletons back at the turn of the century. I, too, lived in a small, gossipy town, and even the high school culture had its share of secrets and stormy relationships. That could be a start. What next?

Perhaps a more personal touch. My mother came from Lewistown, Illinois, one of the places mentioned in Masters' book. The cemeteries there yielded names and artifacts referenced in the poems. The book's druggist, who sold liquor under the counter during Prohibition, was rumored to be my relative. Then there was geography. The students would probably be aware of the name "Spoon River" if they'd ever traveled up to fifty miles south of our town. On those roads, highway signs announced the name of the river as it meandered back and forth in lazy curves. I could solicit where they had heard that name.

I would bring in some additional epitaphs from the actual book. The class textbook had only two or three poems, but the *Anthology* had a couple hundred from which to choose. Filled with irony and injustice, these tales would entice debate.

Balance was important. I decided to use fifteen poems from Masters' book, plus the three in the textbook. "Anne Rutledge" would be an appealing poem, as she was Abraham Lincoln's love who died before they could be married. Then I would use the story of the town drunk, buried next to the temperance magistrate—the judge wasn't happy. I would add "A. D. Blood" who crusaded against sin, only to find two teenagers using his grave for their nightly tryst. That would give them a laugh. "Fiddler Jones" would be a definite option, because he balanced the sad stories with his philosophy of living life to its fullest. He would also contrast with the reluctant "George Gray." I'd introduce the entire lesson with Masters' introductory poem, "The Hill," and then I'd focus on individual stories. "The Hill" would give voice to the town and the many people who were brought back to dwell in the cemetery and later told their stories as they were "sleeping on the hill."

Finally, I'd need an assessment. I remembered an article I'd read about a teacher whose students wrote epitaphs for themselves in the style of Masters. This seemed like a good culminating assignment. Some of them might balk, but I thought it would be an effective way to underscore Masters' style and spark their own creativity.

This is a powerful lesson, I thought, admiring its smooth connections. I hadn't considered that I carried my own emotions into that classroom. It was February, and these students had been in my class for about twenty weeks, long enough for me to get to know them well. I didn't realize how deeply our relationships would influence my reactions to their poems.

I introduced the Masters' poems several days later. "Today we're going to start on *Spoon River Anthology*, an amazing book of poems with scandalous stories. You'll meet people who could have come from our little town, and you'll recognize some of the places mentioned in the book simply because of where we live."

And so the discussion moved on, and after the first day they were deeply engaged in "dumb poetry." Once we deliberated on some of the poems describing injustice and cruelty, they really began to think "this Spoon River stuff" wasn't so bad.

I asked Buff to read the introductory poem about the various residents who had been brought back to their places on the hill, inhabitants of the quiet realm of death. His deep voice picked up the cadence of the poem and when he finished, there was silence that bespoke a curiosity about what else was coming. We read on, and I asked their opinions concerning the sentences that life had often imposed on these people. They argued about interpretations because Masters had left it open for them to make up their own minds about his characters' fortunes.

As we chatted about Fiddler Jones, Ben laughed, because he could see himself as that free spirit. Living long, doing what he wanted rather than what other people thought he should do, and coming to the end without regrets—that story appealed to him completely.

I could see that Linda was awed by Anne Rutledge. She even picked up on the idea that history might have changed considerably if Lincoln had married Rutledge, as he had planned. Looking at their faces and listening to their voices, I could tell they were caught up in the stories.

Chuck raised his hand when we talked about George Gray. I asked about the viewpoint of the poem and how it might translate into real life. I knew if he answered this question he'd clearly see Gray's dilemma: whether to take a chance or choose a safer route in life. Chuck could be decisive when he understood a dilemma.

"We've all known people like that," he alleged confidently. "Afraid to take a chance." Then he lowered his voice a bit and said, "Afraid to fall in love because the person he loves might … uh … not love him back."

At this point a few people chuckled, and Chuck turned around to a friend and smiled.

"All right, go on, Chuck."

He paused a moment to gather his thoughts, then said, "When you think about it … well, some of us will stay here in Monmouth." A few laughs sputtered around him. "Some because that's what they want. Some, I think, because it's just easier. You know—easier to stay than to go away and leave behind what you know. I think that's what George Gray was like, and it seems like he regretted it. Maybe sometimes it's a good thing to take a chance, to see what's out there. That's all." He grinned at me, and I smiled and nodded. He always volunteered answers in class when he was sure.

Chuck Petersen was one of the most popular and busiest people in the class. He played basketball, ran cross-country and track, and in the summer played baseball. He was ruthlessly competitive in the sports arena, but in the hallways of the school he had a gleam in his eyes, a perfect smile, and a laid-back humor that often came out in one-liners that made everyone laugh. Besides sports, he played in the school band, was a class officer, and planned to go out for the class play, an amazing pre-college résumé. Around me, he was a bit shy, but as he got to know me, he loosened up.

Chuck Petersen

He wanted to go to medical school. I thought he would be an amazing doctor who would also have a humane side, a confident manner, and an ear to listen well.

"Chuck, you may be right. So, what do you think, Sarah? Does Chuck have it right?"

"Sure does. Hundred percent. That's me. Staying right here and lovin' it." Everyone laughed because they knew Sarah would be headed off to college the following year.

"So, Ann, if you were to sum up what this book is about, what would you say?"

Ann cleared her throat. "A summary ... well, it's got a lot of stuff in it—themes, I mean. For instance, there's the small town, and the way people act toward each other, and how they look back on their lives. And you can see how life used to be in a small town in the early 1900s. Not much different than here in 1970, is it? Oh, and an important thing is irony. Right?"

"Absolutely. Remember, too, we talked about Masters' use of free verse and the differences in the patterns and length of the lines. So, with that in mind, I'm going to make a writing assignment. You will write a poem, an epitaph, about yourself in the style of Masters." I paused to let them react and then gently chided them. "All right, stop groaning. It will be due one week from today. Make up anything you want about what your future holds." At the back of the class, a student's hand shot up in the air. "No, put your hand down and let me finish, Ben. You can talk about how you died or not mention it, but the most important thing is that you must reveal—and I repeat—you *must* reveal a point of view about your life, just as Masters' characters did. Give the poem your own name, just like the poems in the *Anthology*."

Immediately Rebbie's hand shot up. "So, Mrs. Van Kirk, how long does this have to be?"

"Minimum twenty lines. Oh, and for you, Liz, maximum of fifty lines." Everyone, including Liz, laughed.

Another hand was in the air. "So does the rest of the class get to read these?"

I thought for a moment. "No, but if I'd like you to share yours with the class, I'll ask your permission first, and if you'd rather not, that's okay."

"And we can make up anything we want?"

"Absolutely," I replied. "But no crazy stuff, like being kidnapped by a flying saucer." The bell rang and they took off. I had set in motion an assignment that would be wildly successful, and I would remember it for the rest of my life, but not for a reason I would ever have guessed.

At the end of the following week I collected the poems from the class. As I glanced through them, it was obvious that some had spent a lot of time on them, and others told a good story but had no viewpoint about their lives. That evening I sat down to read them.

The first was an epitaph from the Saunders boy.

Johnnie Saunders

I was the best drag-racer in town.
My souped-up Chevy could take any car
And Anita Sims was impressed with
      my hot ride and strong arms.

One Friday night at the old bridge road
Tom Conover challenged me to a two-mile run.
Stupid punk.
He should have known I wouldn't back down.

We raced from a standstill, neck and neck,
      my Anita by my side.
Then, wheels slammed into each other
And my Chevy went over the bridge railings.
Flying through the air, we landed far
      below in a creek bed.
She was paralyzed for life
And I lie here in this place.

So tell me:
Why do cars and women always screw up your life?

I laughed out loud. This sounded exactly like Johnnie, who'd never met a car he didn't like—or a woman. He spent a lot of time working on his own car on the weekends and talked about it incessantly in his papers. His poem, however, was not bad.

Then there was Samantha's:

The Education of a Teacher

Samantha Thompson

I was five when I first saw my dad beat my mom.
My brother was sick and she was late putting dinner
      on the table and he came home drunk.
He slammed his fist into her nose.
Blood everywhere.
I hid under the table.

After that I stayed out of his way.
"Stupid bitch," he'd call her and hit her again.
But later on when it got quiet and he'd slept it off
I could hear them talking softly in their room,
      she promising to do better.
Of course, that truce didn't last long.
And I swore, "I'll never live like that."

So I made my heart like steel.
As soon as I could get out, I did.
Lots of times guys asked me on dates, but I always
      made an excuse.

Years went by and I realized I was lonely.
So one day I said yes.
Harry and I married and had two kids.
But life was hard and one day he lost his job.
      The bills came due.
      The pressure mounted.
Then one night he came home drunk and hit me.
"Stupid bitch," he said.
I looked at my son cowering in a corner.

That night, once Harry finally went to sleep,
I took my son and daughter from that house.
I never looked back.

My God! I thought. *If this poem is even half true, things are worse than I realized.* I thought about how this kind of abuse had affected Samantha and others like her. Too many of my kids came from difficult family situations. The town was economically depressed, and often homes were like huge pots boiling over on the stove. Unpaid bills were a way of life. Abuse followed. I made a mental note to talk with the counselor on this one and also to sit down and have a chat with Samantha after school.

The next night I slouched my way home after a long and tedious day. I ran a warm bath, submerged myself, and read epitaphs. Some in this batch were depressing and sad. The students poured out their dreams, their frustrations, their sadness, their loneliness. Were any of the characters in the poems happy? A few. But many of them had written of life treating them harshly. Teenage society. Cliques. Abusive homes. Claustrophobic Midwest winters.

However, as time went by and spring was upon us, the winter doldrums and their poems left me, and I forgot about the intensity of that assignment. I had asked a few of the writers if I could keep a copy of their poems. I thought I might use some as examples if I wrote a paper or made a presentation at an English conference. So I threw them into "the black hole," where I stored piles of papers and tests, and forgot about them.

Two years went by, and, on a Saturday night right after Christmas, I put my two-year-old to bed and sat down to read the local newspaper, the *Daily Review Atlas*. My eyes were drawn to a headline on the third page: "Two Monmouth Residents Hurt And Man Killed." I started to glance through it and then stopped cold. I went back to the beginning and read more slowly:

A Sherrard man was killed and two Monmouth residents were seriously injured in a head-on crash Friday at 7:10 P.M. on U.S. Rt. No. 67, a quarter of a mile north of Preemption, according to a report from state police at Rock Island. Route 67 was the main highway north between Monmouth and the Quad Cities—about forty miles of bad road. It was two-lane, hilly, and had few passing spots. Just north of Preemption was a broad curve that hugged a cemetery.

> Killed in the accident was Edward J. Brasmer, 29, of Sherrard, and critically injured were Charles B. Peterson, 20, and Miss Kathy Johnson, 19.

Shocked, I dropped the paper on my lap. Could this be the Chuck I knew? His last name was spelled "Petersen," but maybe it was a misprint. I knew a Kathy Johnson, too, from Monmouth, and I considered what I remembered about her. She had been in one of my classes several years earlier and had graduated just last year. Kathy was tall and slender, with long, dark brown hair. I remembered watching her walk down the hallway with a couple of her friends, books in their arms, miniskirts showing their long legs, like all the other high school girls. As I walked home for lunch one day, I'd watched another student take Kathy's picture in the park nearby for the class officers section of the yearbook. She'd also been at school dances where I'd chaperoned. Kathy was a popular kid.

Kathy Johnson Glasgow, senior photo, 1973

I picked up the paper and looked back at the story.

> Brasmer was going south on 67 and Peterson was going north, according to the report, when Brasmer swerved into the wrong lane and the cars collided head-on. Both cars were almost demolished, and it took some time before Peterson and Miss Johnson could be extricated from their car and they were then

taken to the Moline Public Hospital, where they were placed in the intensive care ward.

A report from the hospital in mid-morning indicated both Peterson and Miss Johnson were still listed as in critical condition. Brasmer was believed to have been killed instantly.

I sat in the chair and just stared at the paper. Chuck was away at college, but probably he was still home on Christmas break. It had to be the two kids I knew. I wondered what they were doing on that road that evening and if the driver in the other car had fallen asleep. Agitated, I got up to grab my phone and then realized it was late, and there was no one to call who would even know anything. So I turned off the lights and went to bed, knowing that I would toss and turn restlessly, wondering what news the morning would bring.

On Sunday morning I started calling friends, picking up whatever crumbs of information I could get. There were few, but I had been right: it was the Chuck and Kathy I knew. Along with me, the town seemed to be waiting to learn the outcome of the accident. And I thought about Chuck, his sometimes serious face and his smile and

Play rehearsal, May '71. Chuck is in his letter jacket, white sleeves

chuckle. I saw him playing the vice principal in the play I'd directed of *Up the Down Staircase*. He had made a great administrator in his gray three-piece suit, carrying himself with authority and dealing out punishments with a grave expression to his friends in the play's cast. In my mind I could see him playing sports, with the tall, lean body of a basketball player and the endurance of a cross-country runner. I could picture him up on the balcony in the gym, playing his trombone in the pep band. Then he had said something, and the whole brass section had exploded in laughter.

Chuck played the trombone in the middle, top row, of pep band

And I cried.

Kathy Johnson had also been in my class during her sophomore year. She was a quiet, slender brunette and sister of Sandy. She'd been a good student, and I'd lost touch with her after high school. I kept thinking about the two of them. I did a lot of deep breathing and tried to go on with household chores and toddler watching. But despite the list of things I needed to do, I found my thoughts returning to the newspaper story, always with a sense of anxiety.

Later on Sunday I got a phone call from a friend. Kathy was still in the hospital but her condition had been upgraded. Chuck, however, hadn't made it. I couldn't force my mind to think or my voice to say, "Chuck's dead."

The following day I read the obituary in the local paper. Chuck Petersen, age twenty, premed student at Southern Methodist University, had died as a result of his injuries. Details of the couple's last night together quickly flew through town. Chuck and Kathy had been on the way to a movie.

The memorial created by the Herluf Petersen family

Later, it became apparent that the head-on collision had been caused by a drunken driver, intoxicated to twice the legal limit.

In the obituary's photograph, Chuck was no longer a boy; he was a man with long hair that had darkened since I'd known him, and he also had a thick moustache and heavy sideburns, typical of the '70s. His fraternity brothers at SMU would be pallbearers at the funeral. The obituary listed many things Chuck had done or accomplished, with a promising career in the SMU chemistry department. He had finished high school with a 4.0 average, was co-valedictorian, and had lettered in three varsity sports. He had continued the perfect grade point average at SMU.

I put the paper down and thought, *What a waste. What a sad, sad waste. Struck down in a moment. To be dead as a result of a drunken driver.* I'd never had a student who had died. Grabbing handfuls of tissue, I tried to staunch the flood of tears. I wished that I could have been able to stop the two of them from being on that road. If I could just rewind that day ... I knew Chuck's parents. I could not imagine what they or his younger brother were feeling. I stared blankly ahead of me, and my thoughts turned to a deep melancholy. I whispered a prayer for Chuck, asking God to be comforting, and also one for Kathy, who was terribly hurt in that hospital forty miles away. They were so young.

I went to the funeral, along with what seemed like the entire town. Chuck's SMU fraternity showed up en masse from Texas, and many of the students who had graduated from high school with him were in the crowd. The family had elected to have an open coffin, and as I walked past it on the way out of the service, I glanced at his face. He wasn't the Chuck I knew. The funeral home had done an arduous job of trying to put him back together, but I told myself he was gone, somewhere beyond that face I didn't recognize. I made it down the short set of concrete stairs to wait outside with a large crowd of mourners. The January weather reminded me of the cold in Whittier's "Snowbound" that penetrated one's bones and could not be kept away by the stoutest coat. The hearse was waiting with the engine running and the doors open. As people filed out and found a place to stand, the family paid their last respects before taking the trip a few blocks across town to the cemetery.

It was a sad, grief-filled ceremony and, as often happens when someone young dies, cohorts of disbelieving and weeping young friends were in the crowd. I hardly recognized some because their eyes were so red and swollen.

I thought of all the times we'd talked in my classes about how authors viewed death, from the rosy descriptions of the romantic William Cullen Bryant, to the macabre machinations of Edgar Allan Poe, to the philosophical renderings of Thornton Wilder in *Our Town*. I thought about *Spoon River Anthology* and the powerful emotions it conveyed about lives torn apart by grief. It had seemed such an academic discussion about death and mourning, one that sixteen-year-olds could not begin to imagine. Now they could.

A few months later, Chuck's father, Mr. Herluf Petersen, showed up at my classroom door, asking for my help in gathering whatever papers he could, papers both touched and written by his son. I felt his sadness all over again. I had thought about the Petersens many times over those cold, early spring days in our tiny Midwestern town. Each time I thought I had chased the sadness away, it came creeping back again, sliding under the cracks of the doors and slithering beneath the loose window frames of my mind.

At the end of that year, as I cleaned out the cabinet I had conscientiously avoided organizing, I found several stacks of *Spoon River Anthology* poems. I remembered then that I had saved them. I thumbed through the copies, seeing names and faces of teenagers who had been in my classes. I paused when I got to Chuck's paper. It had slept in this cabinet for a couple of years, just waiting to be resurrected. I considered calling Mr. Petersen—Herluf—but as I sat back on the cold tile floor of my classroom in front of the messy cabinet and began to read the poem, I knew that I couldn't give this poem to his family—and that I'd never give this assignment again.

He had written it at age sixteen. In the style of Edgar Lee Masters, he had titled it "Charles Petersen."

> I always felt I should pay some rent for the spot I was given in this life:
> > A family that encouraged me,
> > Friends who stood beside me,
> > A brain that should get me on in the world,
> > A competitive body that could play the sports I loved.
>
> And I decided to study medicine and use my talents to pay
> > back what I felt I owed.
>
> So I went to school and studied to be a doctor, passing my
> > exams with ease.
>
> And I set up my practice, doing the work I loved.
>
> One day, while driving to work on the highway
> I rounded a curve and was the first on the scene of a horrible
> > accident.
> > car demolished on the shoulder of the road
> > people in it screaming
> > no one else around.
>
> Of course I pulled over and rushed to help them.
>
> There was a lady, her face and arm bloody and I calmed her
> > and pulled her out through a window,
> > gently laying her on the ground.
>
> Next I went back for the driver.
> And I remember thinking how composed I was and how clear it seemed that I should be here helping them.
> It was the right thing to do.

Just as I stepped into the road, a car rounded the curve
    and drew abruptly on the accident.
The driver, flying around the curve, didn't see me and I took
    the blow full force as I turned to move away.

Rent, you know?

The next day the newspapers called me a hero.

Chapter Six

Past Tense, Future Perfect

In the summer of 2000 I was redecorating a bedroom and traveling around the area, looking for a small dresser lamp to finish the room. I simply had to have the lamp I'd imagined. I happened upon a modest shop one day in Moline that had drapes, hardware, light fixtures, and lamps. Possibilities were endless: bits of fabric samples, lights, wallpaper, and paint. Perfect! I slowly walked around and checked out everything, intent on my quest. An employee glanced my way and then walked over to see if she could help me. There was a flicker of recognition, and I experienced one of those "I know her" moments. She must have had a similar thought because she asked, "Weren't you my high school English teacher?"

I smiled as I realized she was a former student. "I am, and I'll bet you're Emily Finch—is it still 'Finch'?" I swiftly perused a grown-up version of the student I had taught years before. She was a tall, slender woman, with amber hair pulled back and secured by a huge hair clip. Her brown jacket, which draped expertly over her shoulders, looked like it had been made especially for her. She had hints of small lines near the corners of her deep brown eyes, and her skin was a rich olive hue with a trace of color on each cheek. Delicate earrings accentuated her good looks. In all, the effect was that of a successful business owner.

She laughed. "Yes, it's Finch, and it has been since I was in your high school class."

"That was a few years ago, wasn't it?" I replied. "Refresh my memory. Which year did you graduate? Seems to me like it was sometime in the 1970s."

"1971."

"Such a short time ago!" (*At least I was in the right decade.*) In my mind I was calculating that her age must be around fifty. And flickering around the edges of my mind was a darker memory. "How long have you lived in Moline?"

"Well," she began, "I moved here right after high school. Haven't married. No children. But I have a lot of friends. This store's been my life, and I enjoy the buying aspects. Always new shades, colors, different styles. Keeps me hustling." And now her eyes uneasily looked around, as if avoiding my own eyes. I waited to see what she'd say next. She paused a moment, thoughtfully, and shifted topics. "Gee, it's been such a long time since I was in high school. Time flies, doesn't it?"

"Yes, it certainly does."

"Well, enough of my silly musings. What can I help you find?"

When I told her about my lamp quest, she pointed to an area and left me to look while she went to help another customer. A sale was going on, and a number of people were looking for bargains. I had time to think as I wandered through the lamp display.

I had been a novice teacher in 1971—feeling my way along, figuring out solutions to each new problem. I was passionate about my students, classroom, chalkboard, erasers, and even the nail outside the door where I hung my attendance slip. But every so often I still trotted down the hall to ask questions of Phyllis, a colleague.

That year I was in the basement classroom—the one with wooden windows that I had to open and close with a long pole. I couldn't figure out how these windows could leak so much cold air in the winter but also could be so hard to move up and down. My room held five rows of desks, front to back. The north wall was all windows, while the south wall held a clock and a large black cabinet near the doorway. That year, Emily had been in my English class right after lunch. The lazy afternoon sun and the closeness of a basement room in the old brick building conspired to make students sleepy—some of them anyway. On the day I was remembering, Emily—fourth seat by the window—was struggling to keep her head up. I remembered it was fall because we always talked about short stories during the first quarter. I called on Emily, but she absently shook her head.

A few minutes later I noticed she had actually put her head down on her desk; this wasn't like her. I went on with the lesson, considering whether I should say something to her, but I didn't. Later in the lesson, the students read silently. I wandered to the back of the room, and sure enough, Emily was sound asleep. Andrea, one of her friends, caught my eye and motioned me over to her. With a worried look on her face, Andrea pointed at Emily and whispered, "I think something's wrong with Emily."

"What do you mean?" I whispered back. "Do you think she's sick?"

"Well, kind of," she said, her eyes looking at the floor.

"Did you leave school with her over the lunch hour?"

"Yeah. I think she's sick."

"Where did you go? What did she do?"

She hesitated before saying, "I think she may have taken some downers."

"What do you mean 'think'? Did you see her do it or not?"

"She'd kill me if she knew I told you."

"Andrea," I whispered, in my quietest yet angriest tone, "tell me what you know. You'll be in trouble with me if you don't, so stop worrying about what Emily might do."

"I ... I tried to wake her up by tapping her shoulder but she didn't even move."

I reached over and touched Emily's shoulder. By now the other students in the class were aware something was wrong—they either had stopped reading and were watching, or they were hiding their curiosity behind their books. The room was quiet as they waited to see what I would do. I felt all twenty-two pairs of eyes trained on my back, as if it held a target. What should I do? I decided to try waking her again—at least it would give me a few seconds to think.

"Emily." I pushed her shoulder a little harder. "Emily, are you all right?" Nothing. Not a word. Not a movement. Her breathing seemed shallow. I tried again to wake her, and she moved her lips a little but continued to sleep. It seemed that every breath was a little slower, but maybe that was just my imagination. My own chest was tightening, triggered by anxiety. Everyone was waiting.

I thought quickly about what to do. I'd never done drugs in college or elsewhere, but we'd had a faculty in-service that actually had been productive. The drug enforcement police had brought in various kinds of drugs and talked about their effects and what we should do if a student overdosed. My calmness amazed me. "Andrea, go up to the office and tell Mr. Pape that we have an emergency. We need an ambulance. Do it fast."

Andrea left to alert the principal, and I leaned down and pulled Emily away from her desk. Her usual lean, lithe body was not quite dead weight, but any grace of motion was gone, as was her recognition of me or where she was. She seemed to gain enough consciousness to understand what I was doing as I urged her to wake up. "Emily, wake up. Stay with me, kid. We're going to walk a bit. I need you to make your feet move. Come on. Stay awake."

She mumbled something, and one of the boys, Brian, helped me to get Emily's arm over my shoulder. He grabbed the other arm and we got her on her feet and slowly moving. We headed down the aisle—hesitant and awkward—then out the door and into the hallway, with the other students behind us. Expectation, curiosity, and anxiety—everyone was worried, and everyone was wondering what would happen next. I glanced behind us hoping to see the principal. No such luck.

She was conscious enough to help us keep her feet moving a little, and I kept repeating to her various renditions of "Emily, stay with us. Keep moving. Move your feet. We have to walk here. Help's on the way. Listen to me. Try to stay awake."

I don't know why I continued talking except that it seemed to keep a thin thread—a lifeline—between us. I was so afraid—afraid that any moment, Emily might stop breathing and collapse. Perhaps she realized, even subconsciously, the fear in my voice, although I was trying to stay calm.

She mumbled something unintelligible, but she kept her feet slowly moving. Brian was talking to her too as we inched our way down the hall. Finally, Mr. Pape showed up with Andrea and assured us that an ambulance was on the way. He looked down the hallway at the expectant faces and said in a clear, crisp voice, "Go, go, go. Now. Shoo. Head back to your rooms!"

He thanked Brian and took his place next to Emily. Together, we kept Emily on her feet. Brian slid to the floor in the hallway, and I flashed him a grateful smile. Because my room was near the front entrance, we could hear the sirens as they approached; we heard them getting louder and then stopping in front of the school. The principal sent Brian to direct the ambulance workers downstairs, and in a few minutes they were in our hallway with a wheeled stretcher, followed by an anxious office secretary.

When they transferred Emily to that stretcher, I realized for the first time how weak and tired my shoulders felt. I was so grateful that she was still breathing and that people who knew what they were doing were in charge. I whispered, "Thank you, God." They checked her and asked me if I knew what she had taken. I relayed what her friend had said and then watched as they whisked her away.

Finally, the principal thanked me and mentioned something about accident reports and then I went back to my classroom. We didn't finish discussing English that day. Instead, I took the opportunity to listen to their questions and talk to them about what they had seen. I tried to calm their fears and assured them Emily would be all right.

That had been thirty-some years ago—in the early '70s, when drug use was becoming more visible in our students and unsafe stuff could be bought on the streets.

A week later, Emily returned to class, but we didn't talk about what had happened. In fact, she avoided my eyes. I knew from the principal that she was getting help, and I'm sure it took courage to come back through my door. If she had approached me about her problems or the drug overdose, it would have been all right, but I wasn't going to press her. I never brought up the subject, but I often wondered what was going on behind her solemn, deep brown eyes.

Now, here we were in her store, thirty years later. Did she remember that day? And if so, did she remember it as clearly as I did or that it had happened in my class? And what did she think of it now?

My mind returned to the shop and the lamp that I found on sale in the small corner display. A woman was finishing a purchase, and a couple of people came up behind me as I set the lamp down on the counter.

"Oh, this should be perfect for what you described," Emily said. "I'll wrap it."

I paid her. I was aware that the eyes of other customers were on me, so I kept my comments short. "Thanks. I'm sure I'll come back again. It was wonderful to reminisce with you. Such a lovely place you have here."

She handed me the package and then turned to the young clerk beside her. "Matt, this lady was my favorite teacher in high school." She looked at me intently—I so remembered those eyes. Now they sparkled as she smiled at me and added, "And you know how very much I mean that." Her eyes held mine for a few seconds and then broke away.

I said good-bye and drove home, where I unpacked my treasure. I put the lamp on the table in my new room—humble but effective, it would serve.

I've thought of the many people with whom I have spoken over the years—people who declared that they had considered a career in teaching, but something always had gotten in the way: the fear of a low salary, or a better-paying opportunity, or an unexpected event that changed their minds. Often, those same people described, with genuine frustration, their unsatisfactory, boring careers, and then would add, "I imagine a lot of your days were monotonous for you, too, being a school teacher and all."

"I see what you mean," I'd always sigh. Then I'd add sympathetically, "I can't imagine the stress you've had out there in such a difficult job. My job is, as you say, so quiet by comparison."

Chapter Seven

Great Expectations

Great expectations—I always had them. It wasn't Dickens, however, that led me down the righteous path. It was Julius Caesar. The pathetic tale of my hubris began, appropriately, after a discussion of Shakespeare.

Because many sophomores and juniors in my basic English class read below a sixth-grade level, I used tapes of actors reading *The Tragedy of Julius Caesar*. The class followed along in their books, and the tapes helped them understand the iambic pentameter. Occasionally, I stopped the tape, asked them questions, and had them point out lines that supported their answers. They heard the cadence of the voices and the lines, and the pauses and vocal tones helped their comprehension. The language was important, and it led logically into a character discussion.

One student, Jim Talbott, was a natural when it came to figuring out characters' motives. Whether it was Shakespeare's time or the 1970s, he could decipher what people wanted and why. So when it came to discussing Shakespeare, I gave him plenty of opportunities to answer questions—and he offered me a chance to praise his efforts.

On this particular day we had just finished the dialogue between Brutus and Cassius concerning their motives for killing Caesar.

"Let me get this straight," I said, in my best incredulous tone. "Caesar was offered the crown and he *refused* it? I thought this Caesar was an ambitious guy. Why does he refuse the crown when we all know he wants to be king?"

Jim's hand flew up in the air, and Brian, a third-time sophomore sitting nearby, let out an immense yawn.

"Jim, what do you think?"

"Well, sure he wants that crown. Don't ya know? Like in a checker game. If he could say 'king me,' he would. But he's one of those politics guys. He knows the little people, who don't have nothing, don't really want a king. What would they want with someone to boss them around? They probably hear that all the time at home. He's trying to butter them up, to get on their good side by saying, 'Ah, shucks. I don't want your crown.' And you can see it works because everybody cheers. Wouldn't surprise me if he ended up with the whole shootin' works."

"The whole shootin' works?" I asked.

"Well, yeah. Don't ya see? There's these other rich guys who are worried about him, like Brutus, and those are the guys he's gotta win over. Now that would be a fine how'd-ya-do. If he could get those guys to give him a crown, he'd jump at it in a minute, without even saying, 'Mornin'. How's the wife? And gimme that gold hat if ya don't mind, thank you.'"

At this broad translation of how Romans might have talked, the class laughed, and Jim looked around, beaming, as if he were a professional literary critic.

Jim Talbott. In the 1970s anyone who went to our high school knew Jim's family because multiple siblings went to school ahead of him. He stood at maybe five-foot-five, and his round, pale face showed traces of Slavic origin. His blond hair fell over his forehead and into his eyes. Frequently, he looked like he had slept in his clothes, often hand-me-downs, and occasionally, he had a torn pant leg or a button missing. But he was enthusiastic, ingratiated himself with teachers, and held various jobs that defined his spot in the school community. As a hall monitor and a library aide, he overheard countless conversations, and if you wanted to know anything, you only needed to check with Jim. Despite his spider-like information webs, he belonged to no social group. Cliques were not in his vocabulary, and sports and clubs were not a part of his life. He left school at the end of the day to help with his family's business.

I, too, fell under his spell because he knew how to read people in real life, not just in books. His spoken English was not standard, and his reading ability was not close to grade level. But somehow he had managed to reach his sophomore year and earn enough credits to see graduation within his reach. I understood that his family had a profusion of children, and Jim was way down the line. In fact, I didn't know of any brothers or sisters that had actually graduated ahead of him. Most had dropped out for assorted reasons. But Jim would succeed. I decided to applaud him as often as I could. Maybe if he had more confidence and continued to make passing grades, he would graduate; that was my hope.

Earlier in the year I had assigned a research paper, and I knew Jim would have difficulty, so he came in after school and we discussed his interests. Heavy equipment operation surfaced throughout the conversation, and I stopped at the library to check for articles on that subject. I found a few, and we decided to try it. His rough draft had multiple errors in every line, but with diligence and patience, he worked through them. He turned in a final paper that was acceptable.

Because of that persistence, I believed he could make it to graduation.

I was sitting at my desk after school one day when Jim poked his head in the door.

"Hey, Missus Van Kirk," he said in his familiar drawl. "You busy?"

"Not for you, Jim. Come on in." I got up and gestured for him to sit at a student desk. I sat right next to him. "What can I do for you?"

"I wanna do that speech thing you were talking about in class. You know, that giving speeches stuff."

My brow knit in puzzlement. "Not sure what you mean."

"Last week in class. Remember? About how you can do a speech and go to a contest and talk. I know I ain't much on brains, but I had an idea, and I think I could do that."

"*Aren't*," I corrected him. "*Aren't* much ..." Now don't get me wrong; the idea of taking Jim to a speech contest was absurd. Speech contestants were often a "type": college-bound, extremely bright, with standard English skills—and they went to the contest for several years because it took experience to do well. On the other hand, I signed on to teach everyone: the rich, the poor, the "in" group, the "out" group, the ugly, the athletic, the geeks, the annoying, the beautiful, you name it. My conscience whispered, "You've always believed you must teach everyone, and you also said that anyone could go out for speech contest. Here's where reality calls in your note."

I took a tissue out of my pocket and blew my nose to give myself some time to think. After a moment I managed, "Oh, I understand. You're talking about the speech team and going to a contest in a few weeks. That would take a lot of work." I carefully calculated my next words. "I know you haven't done that before. Did you have some topic in mind?"

His face lit up, and his voice took on an excited tone. "Well, I was in the library working the other day, and I heard the librarian talking to another lady about something called the ERA." He sounded out the letters slowly, as if digesting the sounds and trying to remember the letter arrangement. "Seemed like I should know about this, but I don't know nothing 'bout it at the moment. So I asked her what that was—you know, not trying to be nosey or nothing; I was just curious. And she told me that girls don't get much money when they should be paid to do stuff. And they don't have no rights. This bill called E-R-A is about making that work different. I says to myself, 'I could talk about that.' So I thought I'd come right along to you and ask if that might be an idea I could do for this speech thing."

If I had thought of a hundred topics on which Jim could speak, the Equal Rights Amendment definitely would not have been on the list. "Well, Jim, it would take a lot of work. You'd have to go to the library and find information—like we did with your research paper—and then you'd have to organize it and write a speech. You'd practice it after school by yourself and sometimes with me, and then you'd have to memorize it. Come February, you'd go to the contest with the other kids and give the speech. It would be called an oration. Is that what you had in mind?"

He slapped the desktop with his hand and exclaimed, "Yeah, that's *exactly* what I had in mind! You know, I was thinking maybe you could help me with it. But I'd work hard. I promise you I would. I think I could do this."

I was reaping what I had sown. Now I had to figure out how this would work. It wouldn't be easy. I would have to make sure he didn't embarrass himself, or the school, or, let's face it, me. This personal concern was not my finest moment.

"Okay. I don't have anyone who has asked for oration yet for the contest. If you think you can do this, we'll try it. If you decide, once we get started, that it's going to be too hard, we can always cancel."

"That's a done deal, Missus Van Kirk. You won't regret it. Now when can we get this talk started?"

For the next few weeks we worked after school. Of course, I had other students working on various entries also, but Jim was the one who needed the most help. We found several articles about the Equal Rights Amendment, and I talked to him about the type of information he'd need. Then I sent him home with copies of the articles and a red pen. He came back with mark-ups and we added other parts of the articles to his research. Next, we worked on how to cite his sources and finally, it was time to organize it into an actual speech. Once he decided which points he wanted to use, he wrote out the speech like an essay. It wouldn't run the customary eight minutes—more like five—but he could talk about the basics of the amendment and then, in the simplest terms, why it should be passed.

He would have to memorize it, so we worked on that, and I showed him how to go back to a place in his speech if he forgot where he was. Then he came in, day after day, gave his speech for me, and improved each time. Eventually, I thought he could give a passable speech and use decent grammar. Of course, the worst-case scenario was that he might get a difficult judge who would write ugly comments. That sometimes happened, but we'd have to take a chance.

When the contest was a week away, we had a practice where I talked with him about what to expect from the judges and room monitors. He had both questions and fears.

"You know, I'm already a little nervous. What if I forget the whole dang thing? What if I can't get started?"

"You've given it here so many times that you know the first sentence or two. You're going to give your speech for my English class on Thursday. That will get you used to an audience."

"Oh, no. I didn't stop to think about an audience." His eyes took on a worried look. "How many people'll be at the contest where I talk?"

"Probably only a few students. You'll see other contestants in your room and sometimes their friends. They'll just be kids like you."

"Don't think they'll probably be much like me, Missus Van Kirk."

I considered how to answer that statement. I said, "You'd be surprised. The other speakers will be nervous too. It's likely I'll be judging in another room, but if not, I'll come and listen."

"That'd be okay. My folks can't come 'cause they gotta work on Saturdays. No one else can do that for 'em. Have to let 'em know how it went when I get home."

"Sounds like a plan. I thought of another topic we need to talk about too. What are you planning to wear on Saturday?" I slipped this into the conversation with seeming nonchalance.

"Hadn't thought about it. Lemme see. I got jeans. I got a long-sleeved shirt."

"Is there a chance you have pants that are dark but not actually jeans? You know, pants you'd wear to dress up?"

"Don't have nothing that's what you'd call 'dress-up.' Let me think on that for a minute."

I waited through the silence. I didn't want anyone making fun of him or laughing at him for his appearance.

"Maybe my brother has black pants that I think'll fit me. He's a little shorter, but maybe they'd work. And he has black shoes he got last Christmas. That might do. I'll ask my ma about a shirt."

"Sounds good. Jim, no matter how you finish on Saturday, I'll be very proud of you. You've worked so hard."

"I just hope I don't get nervous and forget. You know I never done a speech like this before. It's kinda harder than I thought it would be."

"You'll do fine. Now, come Saturday, I'll pick you up here at the school at 7:00 a.m. The contest is in Galesburg, and this will give us time to travel, check in, find your rooms, and be ready to go. Anything else I haven't mentioned?"

He pondered that for a moment. "No," he said in a quiet voice. "I'll just practice more."

Saturday morning dawned cold and cloudy. No snow. No ice. This year the regional was only about twenty minutes away in my home turf. I had grown up there, gone to the high school, and graduated from Knox College, so I knew the school and probably some of the judges.

I spent the few miles listening to four kids trying to cover their fears with brave talk: Doug, Ann, and Brad were sophomores and juniors, and two had been to contest before. The only silent occupant was Jim, lost in his nerves and decidedly uncomfortable with the rest of the group. They ignored him. He mostly stared out the back window. I asked him a couple of questions and he gave perfunctory answers and continued to stare. We drove the last few miles in silence.

Once there, we headed into the cafeteria to get programs and room numbers. Our little school could fit into this building about ten times.

As Jim took off his coat, I checked out his clothes. He had gotten his brother's pants, and they looked good with the black shoes. His white long-sleeved shirt was a little big on him—the sleeves were wide and gathered at the cuffs—but it was obvious he had worked to look the way he should. It could have used an iron, but it was passable.

"Look at how big this place is. How am I going to figure out where I'm s'posed to go?" He turned the map this way and that.

"Here, Jim. The top of the map is always north." I pointed in that direction and turned the map around so we could see it better. "It looks like Ann is right next door to you, and she's been here before. Ann, could you go with Jim and show him where this room is?"

Ann was a junior and a combat veteran of speech contest. She was dressed impeccably, with every hair on her head in place. A pained expression came over her face, but I stared her down.

"Well—yeah—okay. Come on," she stammered, and then took off with Jim trailing behind.

By now the four had left in search of rooms, and I crossed the cafeteria and walked into the judges room, which was filled with high school coaches and college judges—and coffee and doughnuts. During my high school years, this had been a partitioned area used for the faculty lunchroom, and it held small tables and uncomfortably hard plastic chairs. I grabbed a cup of coffee and sat down to look over the program to see where and what I would be judging. Then I circled room numbers for me and for each of the kids' locations.

"Mind if I join you?" asked a charming, familiar voice. I looked up and saw one of my former college teachers.

"Hi, Professor. Sure, sit down."

"Looks like a good day for a speech contest." He set his coffee cup on the table and sat down. "I didn't realize you were coaching high school speech. My, my. Where are you these days?"

"At Monmouth, not far away. Been there a couple of years. I'm still a rookie at this. I remember speech contest from high school, and oration was my spot." I gave my coffee a stir. "So, what are you judging today?"

"Looks like oration and extemp speaking this morning and after-dinner speaking this afternoon," he mused. He finished thumbing through the program pages, closed the cover, and set it down on the table. He stirred a little sugar in his coffee and glanced up. "Are you judging, too?"

Oh, my God! Epiphany! It dawned on me that my old professor was going to hear Jim. *Think fast, Van Kirk.* Perhaps I should say something to him. Was that ethical? Probably not. No, I should keep my mouth shut—tightly. But Jim would probably not make it past the first few rounds. What was I trying to do here? Give Jim confidence, a pat on the back, an acknowledgement that he can compete and do a good job. Give him an understanding that it's important to be involved, to stay in school. *Should I say something?* I wondered again. The angel on my right shoulder said no, but the devil on my left said yes. I always was partial to that little guy on the left. I drew myself up to a strong posture.

"Professor," I began, "I don't want you to take this wrong, but could I mention a situation that will seriously *not* affect the outcome of this contest? Do you have a few minutes to listen to a quick story?"

He looked at me curiously, intrigued by my question. He glanced at his watch, smiled, and said, "Sure."

I briefly explained Jim's background. The professor listened with an air of concentration, interrupting just once to ask a question, and he appeared to understand my scheme.

"I'm not trying to rig anything or fix anything, but I have to tell you: there is *no way* Jim is going to make it past the early rounds. That's okay. I understand. His competition here is contest veterans, and he doesn't stand a chance. He worked so hard, though, and he really wanted to do this. But what I was thinking was … well … I was hoping you could write him a wonderful critique, and he would have it to remember that he did an amazing job. He got outside his comfort zone." My fingers tapped nervously on my knee. "I know I probably shouldn't tell you this, but as I said, it isn't going to affect the outcome." It was a lame finish, and I looked at him with apprehension.

He stirred his coffee slowly and was silent for a few seconds. My stomach was churning, and I began to think he wasn't going to answer me. I wouldn't have blamed him. He was probably disappointed with me, saddened by my lack of scruples, and let down by my dramatic drop in ethics. Then he looked up and said, "Sure. I don't see why we couldn't do this. It won't affect the standings. Count me in." He smiled and chuckled. "Still trying to transform the world, aren't you?"

I sighed. "Come on, would you expect me to change overnight? But on rare days, even Superwoman needs a little help."

I checked the wall clock and realized it was time to be moving out. I didn't see him again.

Speech contest days were always long. After hearing several rounds, I could tell the best and the worst, but the middle entries got mushy. My brain needed rest. I caught glimpses of my students during the day, but it was no more than a quick look or a brief exchange in the hallway. I was judging when Jim finished his rounds. We all met for lunch and talked over their feelings about their performances. Ann felt she had a chance to go on to the final rounds, but Doug and Brad knew the competition was too good.

And then I spoke to Jim.

"So, how did it go?"

"Well," he began, his tone quickly becoming passionate, "I never heard nothing like it, Missus Van Kirk. These people are so good. This one girl talked about the war in Vietnam, and she said a whole lot of words I never heard of before. And she was excited and very dramatic. I thought, *Wow, I couldn't talk that way, even if I tried rehearsing for a million years.* And I did my speech, and I didn't forget anything. I didn't get stuck in that one spot." He pursed his lips before continuing. "I think I done it my best of all the times we practiced. When I finished, everyone clapped and then it was quiet, and the judge was writing a bunch of stuff. But he did that for everybody else, too." And then without catching his breath, Jim blurted out, "When do we find out what happened?"

I explained that large posters would be put in the cafeteria that listed the people who would go on to the final rounds.

"There's a chance, of course, that you may not make it to the final round. A lot of contestants have been here two or three years, so they have experience. If that happens, go watch other kinds of entries. The acting ones can be very entertaining. And if you do make it into the final round, they'll post the room number and time with the names of the kids who made it. You follow those directions."

"Okay, I can do that. I've been walking around checking out the rooms. Anyway, I think I can find where I should be. You don't have to worry none."

As the day wound down, information about how things were going trickled in a little bit at a time. Jim, of course, didn't make it into the final rounds. When we examined the posters he had finished sixth and seventh out of nine kids in each round. That seemed fine to him because he had not finished dead last. During the afternoon I continued to judge rounds, and Jim and the students who had not made finals moved in and out of classrooms, listening to speeches. In the end, we didn't place students to go on to sectionals.

After the trophy ceremony, I collected the critique envelope, and we began the ride home. Everyone was tired but interested in seeing what the judges had said. I gave the thick manila envelope to Doug, and he distributed the judges' ballots. For a while it was very quiet, and then Ann broke the silence.

"I *cannot* believe this!" Her angry voice shook. "This woman was sitting there filing her nails through most of my extemp speech, and she wrote three words on the whole ballot. Can't you do something about this? Protest it or something?"

I considered for a moment. "I'll see what I can do."

"Ah, a judge with a sense of humor," murmured Brad. "He liked the line about the wet blanket near the conclusion."

And the comments went on. As things got quiet, however, Jim took center stage.

"Missus Van Kirk. Listen to this," he said. He read in a halting, stop-and-start delivery. "'Jim, you have real potential as a speaker. Your organization was right on, and your information sources were excellent. As you keep working on your delivery and do more speaking, you will become less nervous and more confident. Think about doing that. I hope you continue to work at this.'" Jim's voice went up a few notches, and he thundered to the whole car. "Wow! I was better than I thought. I did beat a couple of people. He said other stuff, too, that made me sound awesome. This is amazing. I did a great job! Hey, this was kinda fun."

Smiling, I listened to his remarks. I figured I would drop the other students off first so I could talk with him alone once we got back to town. As I left the students at their homes, I made them promise to bring their critiques back to me on Monday. I took Jim home last, and sat in the car for a few minutes to talk with him.

"Well, I hope you had a good time."

"Oh, this was an amazing day, Missus Van Kirk. I wouldn't o' missed this for anything. Those judges said pretty nice things about my talks. I must be better than I thought I was. And I learnt a lot from watching those other kids. They were so good."

"So, think you want to do this again?"

He grinned, his eyes opened wide. "Well, it was a lotta work. But I liked doing my talk. Once I got started, I wasn't as nervous as I thought I'd be. 'Course, it ain't nothing that my friends would do. And my brother would tell me—he already *has* told me—I'm nuts. I'd have to think about it."

"I'm glad you had a great time. You know, Jim, you can do anything you set your mind to. You could graduate from high school, and that might open real doors for you to get out of town and see the world."

"You mean like Hawaii or Europe? My buddy John said his cousin went to France, and they speak French there instead of English. Imagine that!" he murmured thoughtfully, as if he were trying to work out a problem. "Maybe I could pick up some of those words in France if I tried hard. I'll have to think on that a bit."

"Well, I enjoyed working with you on your speech. You did a spectacular job, and I hope you realize that you are braver than a lot of other people who would never get up like you did and talk in front of strangers. They'd be afraid to. But you weren't."

He grinned. "I guess I did, didn't I?"

"You sure did. Now I want you to show those papers to your folks and let them know what a great day you had. Then bring the papers in to me on Monday, and we'll talk."

"Okay, and thanks," he said as he pushed open the door. He slid over the seat, hopped out, and turned to shut the door, but he hesitated and leaned back into the car. Smiling, he said, "You know, that was really amazing. Maybe I'll give speeches forever." Then with a quick turn of his head, he slammed the door and headed up the walk.

I started the car and thought to myself, *Yes! This is what it's all about.* I considered what a day it had been. Most of the kids were underclassmen, and this experience would help them the next year. I began to mentally lay my plans for next year's categories and speakers.

What I didn't know at that moment was that I wouldn't be doing speech contest the following year. My life had other turns to take. By April, the band was practicing "Pomp and Circumstance," as they did every spring. Faintly, we could hear the familiar notes of the song floating across the hallway.

I wouldn't be at school the following year because my daughter was on the way. I would spend a year out of the life of school to stay home with my young son and my new daughter.

The August following my year away, I settled into a new semester of teaching Shakespeare, Thoreau, and speech. After all the flurry of early year paperwork, I moved into a routine. Then I remembered that this was the year Jim would graduate.

By mid-September I realized that Jim hadn't stopped by to see me. That seemed strange. Where was he? I figured he'd at least want to talk about how his year had gone while I'd been away. The school wasn't that big, and I couldn't believe I hadn't run into him somewhere. He hadn't stopped by my room either. I went up to the faculty lounge and talked to some of the other teachers.

"Have you seen Jim Talbott lately?" I asked Phyllis.

"Now that you mention it, I don't think I have," she said. "I don't have him in class this year, but I have two of his sisters."

"Guess I'll stop by the office and find out what's going on." I left, with a growing feeling of dread following in my wake. A Rolodex file of student schedules sat on the office counter. I checked the names and saw several Talbotts but no Jim. The bad feeling was increasing in tempo. Next, I walked over to the counselor's office.

There I discovered that Jim had dropped out of school. He'd joined the service instead of finishing school to get his diploma. As I walked back downstairs to my room, I struggled not to cry. What had made me think that by patting him on the back and building up his confidence I could make him do what *I* thought was best for him? He was gone, and I could do nothing about it. I had wanted so deeply to see him become the first in his family to graduate high school. Soothing my pain, I thought, *Maybe he's seeing Europe. Giving speeches on a Paris street corner. About women's rights. In French.*

Years later, I often looked back on those younger teaching days and shook my head at the thought that I could shape my students' futures with *my* vision. I speculated on what happened to Jim after he left for the service and occasionally thought about the day we shared. Did he remember driving home and how eagerly he read the paeans to his ability? From time to time, when I remembered him and thought about dropping him off that day, I struggled with my emotions. I wondered if he, like me, remembered his voice saying elatedly as he got out of my car, "This was something. I think I'm gonna give speeches forever."

"Mrs. Van Kirk?"

I came back to reality—I was seated at my desk, going over grades for the midterm with students in my American literature classes. I looked at the boy standing beside my desk—disheveled hair and a skull and crossbones on his black shirt—and said, "Sorry. I was off in space. Where was I? Oh, yes. You know, if you'd work a little harder and get all your assignments in, you could probably bring this C up to a B."

"You're kidding, right?" He gave me a self-righteous look and then said, "Getting a C is fine by me!"

Great expectations. I sighed, them replied, "Okay, then. C is fine. Go for it!"

He sauntered back to his desk, relieved and vindicated. But even as I heard those pitiful, shameful, inexcusable words leave my mouth—even after rehearsing in my head their curved and rounded message—I still felt the hard, brittle edge of their lie.

Part II

The Middle Years
(1980s)

Chapter Eight

Sabrina Fair

Only once in all my thirty-four years of teaching high school English and speech did I have a student named "Sabrina." When I first saw her name, I was reminded of the movie *Sabrina Fair*. And she was. But my memory of her was not entirely about her beauty.

In our town, back in the early 1980s, "diversity" was not a word in my teaching vocabulary. In fact, I'm not sure I ever had a conversation with other colleagues using that word. Diversity, in the town of Monmouth, meant white faces throughout the school with a sprinkling of black faces and a few faces with shades in between. It was not unusual to begin the year with 120 students in my classes; of those, 115 were Caucasian, four were African American, and one was Hispanic or a mixture of races.

Of course, by 2000 that all changed. The school population still included a few African American families, but a steady increase of Mexican families had trickled into town due to Farmland, a meat-processing facility. Built on the edge of town, Farmland employed increasing numbers of Mexican workers, who migrated to our town and settled in. We were reminded of this meat-processing business because on any given day, the air reeked of the smell from the hog-butchering plant, and smoke plumes filled the sky on the far north side of town, where the main building squatted inside a fenced-in compound.

Over many years, however, diversity of another sort occurred in tiny increments—a number of foreign exchange students from Denmark, Sweden, Japan, Holland, and Germany made the long trek to our town. Some who arrived in our miniscule hamlet of nine thousand inhabitants were from large urban areas in Europe. Many of these visitors blossomed, while others grudgingly adapted. But wherever they hailed from, these foreign students brought an exotic culture to many of our kids, who hadn't traveled beyond the confines of Illinois.

Only once before was there another ethnic group in our school. This had happened in the mid-'70s, when Vietnamese students arrived after the end of that war to seek a safe haven. Several families came, sponsored by churches, to begin a new life in the middle of a country that looked and felt nothing like their own. Unlike the exchange students, they had made a perilous and one-way journey from their homeland. They stayed a year or two and then moved on to larger venues, like San Francisco. So for a brief period, we added a few tiny numbers to the diversity factor of our school.

Unlike the transient Vietnamese families who simply disappeared one day, the exchange students stayed for a year and often kept in touch with some of us long after they returned home. The local service clubs and the American Field Service placed them in our school, and we were well aware that they were in town because the local newspaper usually did a feature story on the "visitors."

My fellow teachers and I began every year by looking over our class rosters. By the time I had taught for ten years, I realized that I would continue to see younger siblings of former students. I would be dealing with distraught parents, happy parents, and nervous parents, but many would be familiar parents. So it wasn't unusual to begin a year with well-known names and faces that I could connect by family resemblance. Even walking down the hallways, I passed students I did not personally know but whom I recognized just by family features that were solidly tucked away in my head.

The typical school year began with student rosters containing familiar names like Carrier and Lybarger and Blum and Britt. We knew just by the names what kind of year it would be. While my class lists looked familiar, I didn't realize in the fall of 1980 that a revelation awaited me in my junior/senior American literature class.

I was up on the latest research about teaching diverse school populations. Intellectually, I knew about issues of diversity, even if I had seldom experienced it. I was sensitive. I had gone to college in the sensitive '60s, when everyone had a point of view, and "conflict management" was a buzzword. Tolerance for other cultures and viewpoints—thy name was me. I was confident and relaxed, usually working hard to help exchange students so far from home feel comfortable and accepted. I was prepared for the first faculty meeting of the year, in which we would find out whether we would enjoy the specific 120 students coming our way, and whether or not we would have a foreign exchange student in class.

You see, the school district withheld our class lists until the day before school began, when we were sitting in a teachers meeting surrounded by our colleagues—and we had nowhere to escape. Tan and rested from the summer, we sat in a tangle of teachers, all of us looking at our class lists, hoping for the best or fearing the worst. In this particular year, my class lists looked familiar as always. There was an Armstrong, a Carrier, a Hallam, several Johnsons, a Talley, a Toler—and a Fakroddin.

Wait a minute ... what was that last name? Fakroddin? *Fakroddin, Sabrina? Doesn't sound familiar. Haven't seen that name before.* Immediately, the neurons in my brain fired up and began the race from mental closet to closet, checking out that name. Nothing here in '75, and nothing there in '79. I could hear the little voices echoing from one neurological location to another. "Nothing here!" Scampering from one yearly closet and rounding a corner to the next, I could almost hear the doors slam shut when no Fakroddin appeared. This seemed highly irregular. Why hadn't I heard this name before? Puzzled, my mind closed the last of the yearly name doors and suddenly came upon a brilliant assumption. She was an exchange student. The last name seemed rather unusual. I decided I would wait to see what this "Fakroddin, Sabrina" looked like.

On the first morning of school, twenty-four expectant faces sat before me in my literature class, all eager to start the school year. New clothes, new binders, new resolves, new potential problems, new hopes … and old names. I knew quite a few of these faces. Some I'd seen before in English classes and others I'd watched on the basketball floor or on the debate team or in school plays. So I began, as always, going down the roster and pronouncing most of the names to everyone's satisfaction. Allison, Anderson, Cavanaugh, Ingersoll, McNamara, Salaway, Weegar, Wright. By now I had decided that Sabrina Fakroddin must indeed be an exchange student. Besides the familiar faces, I saw a young girl with a decidedly Asian look. She was glancing around at the animated faces of her fellow classmates but looking very much alone. She might have been about my height—five foot four—and was very slender with small shoulders and delicate features. She appeared to be Indian or Pakistani, but whatever she was, she was not the usual student in our little town.

Sabrina Fakroddin Smith, 1981

Although she was dressed like my other teenagers, her features were nothing like theirs. Her hair was a dark, glossy black and hung to her shoulders in a relaxed and slightly wavy curl. She had brown eyes that looked out at the classroom nervously. What really set her apart was her smooth olive skin, beautiful by any definition. Her eyebrows, eyes, nose, and mouth didn't resemble any siblings I'd ever had, nor did her features seem typical Monmouth ethnicity or race. Within a sea of white faces, she was extraordinarily lovely, with perfectly symmetrical features and with the heightened contrast of dark eyes set against her beautiful complexion. I must have been staring because I suddenly realized she was uncomfortable, and she lowered her eyes to the far left corner of the notebook on her desk.

I decided I would wait to butcher her name at the end of my roll call. That way I could ask her how to say it correctly and also add a few welcoming words to make her feel more comfortable. She was probably anxious, feeling as if she had been set down in the middle of a God-knows-where cow town and wondering if there might be a graceful exit to a place where there were bright lights and tall buildings.

I'll bet she's from India and speaks English as her second language, I thought, smiling. *So how should I deal with that?* I decided she probably would need my patience, understanding, and exceptionally slow, carefully articulated speech. I walked toward her—second desk in the left-hand farthest row. I stood right in front of her, knelt down slightly, and said very slowly, in infinitely patient syllables with moderate decibels, "My ... name ... is ... Mrs. ... Van ... Kirk. You ... must ... be ... Sabrina. Where ... are ... you ... from?"

She looked up at me, smiled brilliantly, and answered in a clear but equally sluggish speed, "Spring ... field."

Chapter Nine

And the Walls Came Tumbling Down

No collection of teaching stories about my career would be complete without the bizarre and dark tale of another "friend" during my thousands of teaching days: the high school building. However, I had to enlist some help for this story. It is a tale of madness and mayhem, a struggle between education lost and building gained.

By 1979, like an old car that had 1,000,000 miles on it, the high school building had seen better days. In a practical sense, the building had outlived its time. But beyond the practical, the human brain covers the bricks and wood with layers of associations that plug into sockets of breathing, living memory. Lives happened in that

MHS at the beginning of the siege

building, their sound tracks strongly steeped in the corridors, their coming-of-age memories connected to the pale pink or gray walls and the wood and glass doors. The pulsing drumbeat of "Wipeout" from the band room, the sound of laughter from the biology mouse wing (called "the maternity lab"), the clicking of typewriters in the business rooms, the shrill whistle emanating from the gym—the old building breathed with the sounds of life.

What I remember about the old building was uneven heat, poor lighting, and the cold drafts that came through the sides of the windows. Students would freeze in some classes and sweat in others. Winter frost and snow appeared on the *inside* of the windows, and the light fixtures hung down from high ceilings and cast poor illumination on the desks. The floors were mostly hard tile and the walls were institutional pinkish. Added to this were the much-abused and overused green chalkboards—yes, they were green. The heating, electrical, and mechanical systems, plus the plumbing—just everything—was ancient, and it must have cost thousands of dollars every year to maintain. It wasn't a terribly comfortable place to teach or learn. But often its former students thought of their human memories and forgot about such practical considerations as heat, lighting, and water.

Looking back, those students had conflicting opinions about its nostalgia vs. comfort. Beth McCurdy Swedeen ('81) told me, "I remember the heating system was pretty bad, and my sophomore year, we were the only school district in a fifty-mile radius that didn't cancel school for the cold. But the heat wasn't working, so we all wore our coats all day and didn't really do much work because it was *freezing*! Despite that, I thought it was a great old building. I happened to have a lot of classes in the basement, and, in the spring and falls, we'd sit in the deep window wells with the windows open at grass level with the outside. Sometimes we'd just scoot on out the window and leave at the end of the day or at lunch or after finishing an exam." And Rick Kellum ('83) added, "My impressions of the old Monmouth High School are of a shadowy place with wide, varnished stairways, especially the bottom floor back by the boiler room. I only attended the old school for one year, but it was my first year of high school so the impressions linger, and it's this building, rather than the newer, more plastic-looking one we moved back into, that I find myself picturing as I write my [current] novel."

So what to do about this aging dinosaur? By 1979 it was obvious that we needed a new building, and it would take millions of dollars. The school board had a different idea, a novel plan that was implemented the following year. The 1980-1981 year witnessed the bone-jarring, ear-numbing sound of jackhammers; the smell of dust, sweat, and acetylene torches; and the sight of darkened, cave-like hallways, their air thick with gritty, gray dust. Those of us who spent that time at the high school will remember and share forever those sights, smells, and sounds, and our lungs will also share some of the particles of that building forever. This truly was a year from hell.

A dead fish, the death of culture, and *The Grapes of Wrath* were all part of that school year that caused us to ask the board of education, "Were you out of your freakin' minds?"

But it did have its moments of black comedy. Did I mention the dead fish?

School finances—they were always a tricky issue in education, and our district was no exception. We were surrounded by other districts with no way to acquire land or the money from industries, so the school board came up with a novel way to save money. They decided to "renovate" the building. None of us really knew what that meant, but we were soon to find out. That year provided new opportunities to defy death, suffocate in dust and grit, and listen to six teachers and over a hundred students all talking simultaneously, which resulted in a deafening cacophony.

The old, three-story brick building was the backdrop in my dreams during my early years of teaching. It was shaped like an L, with the top of the L at the south end; the floors running north and south seemed to be the longest. The bottom of the L ran east and west. Fortunately for the bricks-and-mortar skin, the building's brain had no idea of what was about to happen to its skeleton and internal organs.

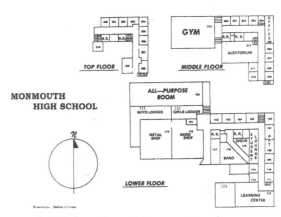

MHS floor plan with renovation changes

To understand the scope of the changes, picture the workers as a ubiquitous army. This army totally overhauled the science labs on the top floor. Below, on the main floor, the offices became larger, and a huge east entrance to the building and its wide set of marble stairs completely disappeared, with new classrooms rising in their place. Another set of stairs on either side of the stage took students up to the auditorium, and the workers closed off one of those stairways and its door. They totally destroyed and rebuilt classrooms and a band/vocal music area in the basement. A tangle of short hallways, weaving in and out of each other, that contained janitors areas, the boiler room, and a faculty restroom completed the basement. All of those disappeared or moved after the renovation, and a new student lounge and an elevator to the auditorium took up much of that area.

This east entrance was closed forever

So how to take a huge, three-floor building apart and still keep school going? The 1980 yearbook, with a section by Dianne Wingfield, explained the process of moving everyone. The classes on the north side of the building moved to the auditorium and east side of the building in early February 1980. The band went to the large all-purpose room, out of the battle area. Meanwhile, the construction crews tore up walls, floors, and ceilings in vacated rooms and hallways. According to Wingfield, "Soon sounds of falling tiles, boards, and plaster were heard, accompanied by dust in the halls and rooms."

Talk about an understatement! The yearbook didn't even begin to describe the human drama of that year.

Students moving between classes near front entrance during renovation

Take the hallways and the dust—I should have been teaching *The Grapes of Wrath*. The raging storms of dust coming across the plains would have left nothing to the imagination when my students were swimming through dust every time they changed classes. One of my most vivid memories was later in the renovation, when I moved to a basement room underneath the main office. Between classes, one of my students, Art Toler, was coming down the hall toward my room, but I couldn't see him. I could hear him laughing and then shouting, "I'm coming, Mrs. Van Kirk, if I can find you!" He was fifteen feet away, and neither of us could see the other for the dust.

The dust was everywhere. That year I had a classroom set of dictionaries with hard-back covers. For five years after the renovation we still used those dictionaries. This often prompted my students to ask why they were all gritty.

And other people were out in those hallways too.

Bill Pieper, biology teacher, remembered his year: "I know I would come home, and my clothes would go in the laundry each night, and on top of my shoes there was thick dust everywhere. And, ah, the grand old building. It was so solidly constructed that when they tried to drill holes in walls they broke drill bits constantly. When they got to the basement, those walls were three feet thick. The drills broke because the walls were laced with rebar [rods of iron all through the foundation to add reinforcement]. Asbestos was in the tiles and mortar. Looking at the photos, you can see the groove rings in the ceilings, and they just scraped those down. Dust was everywhere as they cut through those walls. Because this building was constructed in 1910, there had to be asbestos throughout the building, and that dust probably added bulk to our diets that year! We had chemistry lab up on the third floor with live gas mains when they were working just below us. They wouldn't let us do that today. So many laws are in place now for life-safety issues. They'd force us to be out of there."

Bill Pieper, king of the biology lab

Darkness, open fixtures, lower hallway

And there were other safety considerations too. Pieper described the scene outside his door: "One of the amazing things was that there weren't more accidents or people hurt. Right outside my lab [third floor] was a nonstop tube right down to the basement and an open shaft where you could see down three floors. There was just this piece of plywood across there and numerous ways the kids could have gotten into trouble throwing stuff down there but they didn't."

Students were out in those hallways and many of them described the conditions from that year. Ronda Ehlen Willhardt ('81) mentioned, "All of my books were covered with

Three floors straight down

grit. Girls that sprayed their hair found their hair quickly covered with grit and dust, sticking to their hairspray. The desks and lockers were also covered with grit. The basement hallways were cave-like, with open bulbs in the ceilings, scaffolding we had to walk through, and floors we couldn't sit on because of all the dust and dirt." Then there were the lowered ceilings in the hallways and the workers. Nancy Gilson

Students passed around scaffolding like this

Inness ('81) noticed, "There were blue chalk lines in the halls because they were putting up the lowered ceilings. I was amazed at how they did that. And I remember miles and miles of open ductwork. The workers' equipment, scaffolding, tiles, and dust were everywhere, and they drew chalk lines on the floors. I also watched the construction guys up on scaffolding in the middle of the hallways. The girls, of course, were checking them out. I always remember thinking these guys have to be pretty brave to stand on this scaffolding while students are passing around them in big bunches. In the basement I can remember at least an inch of water all over the floors. I walked out of Spanish class thinking, *Look at these electric cords all over. This has to be dangerous.*"

I wasn't in the basement very much during the early phases, but Jean Ann Stewart Burgland ('80) remembered, "The basement floor was the worst. Looking back I'm really surprised they even had us walking through all the sawdust and wires and the contractors' equipment, materials, and tools."

At this point you might be asking yourself—between coughs and wheezing—why did we do this? Why not build a whole new building and then move us into it after it was all done? Enter the principal, Clyde Farwell. "When I took the principal's job at MHS in 1975, there was talk even then that they would build a new high school, and that was one of the things that interested me about the job. I thought it would be a real challenge to build a new building. But that wasn't exactly what happened. District 38 had just come out of deep financial problems and it was time to deal with the bad shape of the high school building. The heating system was just not adequate. We had trouble keeping the system up

Mr. Clyde Farwell, principal

and going in the winter and some sections of the building couldn't get much above sixty-two if it were a zero degrees day outside. Unfortunately, to build a new building would cost millions, and we would need a transportation system since it would have to be built in the southwest part of the district. So we hired a firm to assess whether the current building was structurally sound. And it was.

"Supt. Stanton did a very smart thing: he borrowed money ahead of the renovation, at a time when interest rates were about 12-15 percent. So he was able to invest and get a huge return which would, in effect, give us more money than we bonded for. The tax referendum passed for $2,063,000, and Stanton's investment gave us something like four or five million that we were able to put into the building. The people of the town passed a referendum to do it. But then we had a whole new set of problems. How did we have school while all of this was going on?"

And so the Steinbeck moment began with drills and flying dust everywhere. The hallways were always an adventure. But the auditorium was sheer student entertainment. The administration had to decide where to put these six hundred fifty-plus students while the basement was being torn up. They decided to use the auditorium for six classrooms, and I was one of those teachers, along with others from English, math, and social studies. Sounds simple, right? No one could ever have predicted the chaos we would be going through in trying to teach in these conditions. It was built-in attention deficit disorder.

Nancy Gilson Inness told me, "I was a junior during the winter construction and had American literature in the auditorium. First, they removed all the seats. Then they put a hundred-plus desks in the auditorium, figuring to have classes there. We were there for a week when someone asked if the floor would hold all this weight. So they stuck us some other place and had the engineers check it out. Finally, they moved us back in when they decided the floor would hold. They also put in partitions that were about six feet tall and placed plastic sheeting over the top like a ceiling; they laid the plastic on top of ropes.

But the fire marshal said they had to remove this plastic, leading the way for students to throw all kind of projectiles (like coins and paper planes) over the partitions. There were six classrooms, three on each side, from the back of the auditorium to the front. Down the slope, back to front, was walking space. And this 'hallway' on either side went past each of the three rooms, whose fourth side was totally open to the people walking by."

Attention spans in the auditorium were hampered by both flying missiles and other classes. Ronda Ehlen Willardt explained, "The most interesting classes were in the auditorium. The boys built arsenals of flying weapons and synchronized their watches with military precision so all projectiles went over the partitions at the same time." Rick Kellum added, "I had algebra in one of those partitioned classrooms with Mrs. Wheeler. Of course, Mrs. Willhardt also had a class there at the same time, next partition over, and she spoke so loudly she drowned out Mrs. Wheeler. So I sat there and listened to Mrs. Willhardt talking to her honors English class about the movie *Airplane!* and how it used bits and pieces of other movies for its jokes. She must have been explaining parody or satire. I found that class far more interesting than algebra."

Auditorium classroom of Phyllis Wheeler.
Rick Kellum far right, dark hair.

Other teachers in the auditorium were having difficulties simply teaching. Ron Murphy, social studies teacher, said, "The most difficult adjustments in the auditorium were showing movies and doing my various simulation games. It was never dark enough for films, and the game-playing had to be a nightmare of noise for those classes around me. By the time the renovation was done, I had five different classrooms in two buildings, which included one or two spaces in the makeshift auditorium."

My own recollection of that teaching year in the auditorium was that for a person seriously trying to teach, it was like doing so in one of Dante's rings of hell. First, the noise was deafening from six classes all talking at once, and you couldn't hear anything, including yourself. And some teachers who had little control over their classes just increased the noise to a higher roar. The discomfort of standing on a floor that was pitched at an angle got very old, and student desks were constantly moving down the sloping floor, sliding toward each other, making it difficult to give tests. We were right over the area where they were destroying the band room, and the constant hammering was so loud you couldn't hear, and the smell of various chemical gasses found its way to our miserable classrooms. This is what a typical discussion in my "room" sounded like:

Me: "Okay, open your books to—" (The sound of jack hammers drowns me out so I stop talking. Three minutes later the jack hammers stop.)

Me: "—page 235 and look at the first paragraph. How did Steinbeck introduce his—" (The sound of jackhammers starts. Jackhammers end after five minutes.)

Me: "Okay. That was page 235. How did Steinbeck introduce the themes of his—" (Jackhammers start again and stop after three minutes.)

Me: "—short story in the very first paragraph of the piece? (Hands go up.)Yes, Brian?"

Brian: "I think he foreshadows the idea of death by—" (Jackhammers start again and stop after two minutes.)

Me: "Go on, Br—" (Jackhammers start and stop after five minutes.)

Me: "Dear God, will this infernal noise ever stop?" (But I'm thinking, *"This is only January, and we have how many more months of this? Illegal or not in school—dear God, please let them break another drill bit that has to be ordered from far, far away! Then let the UPS trucks break down or the post office lose power.)*

I sigh.

"Okay, get out a sheet of paper, and I'll put a question on the board for you to answer."

It was totally impossible to teach anything that involved speaking—like literature discussions—so students did a lot of writing, the one skill that did show improvement.

Of course it was virtually impossible to use any kind of technology, such as overhead projectors, because of the lighting situation. So you had your textbook, a makeshift chalkboard, long pauses for hammering, and that was about it.

But it had its comic moments. Where else could you be teaching *The Old Man and the Sea* and suddenly, a dead, smelly fish would come flying over the partition and into your classroom, hitting three students on its way to the floor? One of the students picked it up and threw it back, the opening gambit in the "War of the Flying Fish," followed by appropriate screams throughout all six classes as students were hit and returned fire. The principal observed, "Student attendance that year was the best it had ever been during my tenure. I suspect students felt the building renovation was very entertaining."

Score one for entertainment, but learning was certainly not on the scoreboard. As time went by I became more and more desperate to find a situation where my students could actually learn. So after the fish fiasco I decided to try a different tactic.

I begged, pleaded, and generally visited misery on Mr. Farwell to let me go to a room where I could shut the door and teach. That was how I became sole owner of the northeast basement corner of the building. I was still around jackhammers and thick, choking dust, but I had a door on my room and no other classes nearby. What luxury! Finally, we were safe. It was still noisy but the door muffled the jackhammers better because they weren't right below us, and we no longer had the cacophony of six classrooms with bare wooden floors and a tall ceiling to project all the noise. I was in heaven—well, relatively speaking.

A basement room demolished

Now we could actually talk about Mark Twain and Flannery O'Connor, and as days went by in the basement room, I began to feel like some normalcy had returned. The problem of occasional falling plaster and gritty, dusty desks still greeted us every morning, but at least we could hear ourselves think despite the somewhat distant jackhammering.

The overhead lights in this room were different from the lights in my "old" basement room that hung down on long poles. In this room the lights were in double bays of silver metal that hung down the entire length of the room. Metal pieces crisscrossed the two-foot width of the lights about every six inches, and they hung only a few inches from the ceiling. My students' desks likewise ran the length of the room in six rows. We got used to plaster occasionally falling down, but one unforgettable day—between jackhammer bursts—an entire light bay went crashing to the floor, raising dust and debris and throwing electrical cords and metal in every direction. This totally unexpected horror caused everyone to jump and scream, including me. In fact, it probably created many religious conversions, as the entire bay of lights fell to the floor exactly between two rows of desks that were filled from front to back with students. Miraculously, no one was hurt. Once everyone calmed down, including me, I sent a student to the office for Mr. Farwell. Luck was again on our side, but no one doubted after this that even though everyone was doing what they could to keep us safe, the building was a scary place for all of us.

Mr. Farwell reflected, "The conditions were really severe, and you teachers had a union and if you wanted to call a spade a spade and say these were unsafe working conditions—which they were—then I'm not sure what would have happened. And the longer we went on with the tearing down, the worse it got."

People in other parts of the high school were having interesting days of their own. Richard Brett ('80) said, "I remember in particular the destruction of the old band room and the sort of lawlessness that arose from it. One day we were all milling about in there, and Danny Queen found an old viola or cello and, with a scream of delight, smashed it on the floor as the rest of us looked on. *Culture at MHS is now dead,* I thought."

During this time the guidance counselor, Terry Miller, was in an office away from the auditorium or basement. He told me, "One of my memories of the renovation occurred in my own office [which was a tiny room at the top of a small flight of stairs near the main office]. My desk sat right in front of an air grate. And through the air duct I could hear the workers talking, cursing, etc. One day they were demolishing the duct system and suddenly, through the duct, came a huge cloud of black soot that covered me, my desk, and the room in dirt. I didn't have time to escape."

Bill Pieper was having difficulties of his own up on the third floor: "We science people remained on the third floor so we could set up classes that needed labs. The only room that got torn out was a catch-all room that eventually became the opening to a stairwell that went down three flights to the learning center. They tore it all out while I was teaching, and huge plastic drapes were hung behind us so you could hear the construction going on but be somewhat away from it, even though the dust would come under the plastic. But the kids did a wonderful job maintaining their concentration during the adversity of tearing out this room.

Plywood covering a dangerous drop on the third floor

The one time they were really distracted—so was I—was between what was fourth and fifth periods. I'm lecturing and I hear this 'Oh, hell of a shot!' And then a little pause, and then a crash, and 'Oh, damn!' And then there would be another pause, a crash, and, 'Oh, man, what a hell of a shot!' So I went out, and here were two of the construction guys. They had used a brick to hold down dollar bills, and they were dropping cement chunks into five-gallon buckets three floors below because there were no steps in there yet, so it was a straight, three-story shot. They were on their lunch break. Later, I had a word with their foreman and the game of chance moved elsewhere."

In the teachers' minds the questions truly were did education win this year? Did anyone learn anything? The teachers taught valiantly, the students were entertained, and most learning went out the windows with the dust and fumes. But the district saved cash. And summer vacation finally arrived to the great relief of the teachers.

Finally the tearing-down phase ended, and the actual "renovation" began. I dreaded going back into the building the following fall and evidently I wasn't alone. Parents, teachers, and students exerted constant pressure not to return. Fortunately, Monmouth College came to our rescue and offered us rooms.

One of the difficulties of teaching at the college was that all our textbooks and equipment had to be moved, and teachers were responsible for doing that. This was grueling for a literature teacher with multiple heavy books. And there were no elevators in the building we were using, Wallace Hall. So I had to lug literally hundreds of books up a hill and two flights of stairs to start school at the college. But the rooms were clean, and there was no constant noise and no dust! Amazing! We taught from noon until five.

The high school building was still not done after our two weeks at the college. Again, the college graciously offered us their buildings for another four weeks. When we finally returned to the high school in October, we used only the upper two floors because workers were putting false ceilings in the basement areas and finishing up the band room. They completed the building renovation by the following March. I remember this phase of the process as being relatively benign compared to the past winter, because they were building rather than tearing down. Now it was hammers and electric drills, compared to jackhammers. A cinch!

Looking back on that year, most teachers and students alike would agree that the atmosphere of the building totally changed because of the renovation. The old building had huge wooden windows and doors with glass transoms; it could in no way be called modern. Many of the rooms on the main floor contained oak cabinets and glassed-in shelves for books. The hallways and the floors were combinations of wood and tiny white/black art deco tiles that covered parts of the walls up to shoulder level. Near the main office was a student office where Student Body Association tickets were sold for various events and students often gathered. That was now gone.

The new building was so much cleaner looking with lowered ceilings, strategic lighting, and colorful chalkboards and bulletin boards. It was much brighter and the colors were no longer that dull, institutional neutral. And it was safe. Everyone realized that it was cleaner, brighter, and more conducive to learning. Some students gave it mixed reviews, however.

Nancy Gilson Inness explained, "We had had wooden lockers, and the new ones were smaller and metal. The floors had been beautiful with little octagonal tiles. Now they were large orange squares. Even the clocks on the walls had been beautiful. I feel bad they had to rip all those things out. I always liked the oak woodwork and cabinets, and all of that went." One of her friends, Beth McCurdy Swedeen, spoke of the new building but was in a tough situation herself that year: "I really enjoyed having an old building with lots of character. When we moved back in, all of the cool architectural features were gone (marble steps, deep windows, wood trim). They got rid of open lunch (ostensibly, they didn't want people spilling food on the new carpet). During all of this, my dad was on the school board, and he had no time for anyone who complained. I sort of remember seeing his point of view and being loyal to the board decision because he thought they were doing the right thing to save energy and costs. In retrospect, I think they ruined a great old building."

The "new building" had a lot more plastic and bright colors. This prompted opinions from students like Marjorie Allison ('81), "I loved the history of the old building—the old wooden lab tables and the glass bookcases in the chemistry room, the sense that lots of students had used the building in the same way I was. I think I remember wooden lockers before the renovation, at least in parts of the building—and I liked them—nice and big. In fact, my first locker in the building was on the first floor and had 'Stuart Allison' written in it. And I think [my brother] Stuart and I determined it was left from my [uncle] Stuart's time in the building, not my brother's. The new tile floors and the new paint? Not my choices!" Ronda Ehlen Willhardt added, "I remember feeling the new building was much more sterile. The textures were gone."

None of us dreamed that a building renovation would resemble going into labor with your first child: no matter how much you swear about the pain, once it starts you don't have any choice about letting it take its course. You couldn't say, "Wait! Stop! I'm not ready to do this!" The primitive conditions meant honing our teaching skills to the very basics, without technology or the ability to move furniture or students into groups. After all, Socrates taught with questions only. However, his voice didn't have to compete with jackhammers.

Looking back, I just shake my head as I think about the novice teachers in that building. No amount of college preparation could have prepared them for that human comedy. How could they have had any idea of the problems they'd encounter while teaching in a battle zone? On the other hand, we all realized the school district was attempting to do its best to save money.

These money-saving measures happened long before the troublesome lack of federal funding for No Child Left Behind. My colleagues during that dust-driven year understood the financial necessity, but they wondered why schools must continually find ways to cut, dice, and chop because they are always at the end of the line for the meager leavings of the tax revenue stew.

Those of us who taught through this horrific year found a camaraderie that extends to this day. The idea that we could somehow teach through this dust-choking, jackhammer-jarring year in our lives amazed even us. The battle stories are a part of the history of the building and the people who passed through it. While it had its comic moments, it also left us with a feeling of having been tested and survived, teachers and students alike.

Nancy Gilson Inness summed it up this way, "In the long run it showed how you can do anything if you put your mind to it. We muddled through. It's amazing when you think about all those kids that year—*Us*! Amazing that we survived!"

Chapter Ten

Transitions

Suddenly the doorbell rang, causing a hit of adrenaline and jolting my frayed nerves. I had been playing a game with my six-year-old on a frigid Christmas-break day. I needed some rest and some "down" time, so this was going to be a good two weeks when I could get away from my teaching and just enjoy my children. Outside, icicles dangled from the front porch overhang, and tiny specks of salt lodged between the ridges of the ice on the sidewalk, waiting for that catalyst—sunshine. Even our two-story house on East Broadway felt chilly, as if it were shuddering in the gray December light, and when the doorbell rang I wondered who could be out on such a bitter Saturday morning. I left Steve in the toy room and smoothed down my hair on the way to the front of the house. Turning the old-fashioned skeleton key we always left in the lock, I looked out into the white glare. On the porch, shivering, stood one of my students.

"Wendy!"

"Hi, Mrs. Van Kirk. Sorry to bother you at home because well, I'll bet you're busy." Her anxious eyes stared at me. "Hey, if you're busy, you know, I could come back another time."

Wendy Stowe—disheveled hair, dark circles under her eyes, and a trickle of mascara that had dried below her left eye. Usually, Wendy was a portrait of flawless style: long, strawberry-blonde crinkly hair and light blue eyes. But now, waiting on my porch, she shivered as vapor escaped from her chapped lips.

"No, this is a perfect time. Good grief, it's freezing. Come in." Grabbing her by the arm, I pulled her into the house as my foot pushed a couple of Steve's toys out of the path into my living room.

"I've been kind of … well, I … I heard from Mindy that you lived near the grocery store on Eleventh, and so I decided that I was going for a walk, and I thought I would stop, figure out which house was yours, and … and talk to you."

My two younger children wandered in to see who was at the door.

"It's okay," I told them. "Wendy's one of my students who's just visiting. We're going to talk a bit, right here in the living room. We'll just be right here."

"But the library—what about the library? You said you'd take us," eight-year-old Jen said.

"I will. Promise. We'll go in a little while." Their eyes took in Wendy momentarily, and then they both turned around and headed back to the toy room and *Sesame Street*.

I gestured to the sofa. "Now, come on over here, sit down, and tell me what's happening. How's your Christmas break going? Coffee? I just made some."

"No … no coffee." She slipped out of her shoes and looked around at my living room. "Thanks, anyway … for the coffee."

"Here, let me take your coat." She shrugged out of her coat and scarf and held them out. She was wearing faded jeans, a white-collared blouse, and a sweatshirt that read "University of Utah." While I hung up her coat over the stairway banister, she tiptoed to the couch, and I followed her, picking up a toy xylophone that had been discarded on the sofa cushion. I sat down and waited for her to talk.

"I really like your house," she sighed as she took in the ceiling and walls of my living room. "Blue's my favorite color. And the ceilings—wow, they're so high. And, oh, wow—wooden beams. How gorgeous." Her eyes rested on an oil painting on the east end of the room. "Beautiful. Are those your kids?"

"Yes."

She brightened a little with a tiny smile. Her blonde hair fell into her face, and she brushed it back. "I imagine you had a really good Christmas, you know, since you have your kids here and all," she said. "I always think you need kids around to have Christmas be what it's s'posed to be." Her eyes darted around the room like a sparrow and I wondered, as I listened to her rambling dialogue, why she had chosen to alight on my doorstep on such a frigid morning.

"Well, I definitely have kids—three—although the one who's about to be a teenager is already practicing his sleeping-in." Reaching across her to the coffee table, I straightened out a couple of magazines and a book I'd been reading the night before. "So, I know you didn't stop to talk about my kids. Did you have something on your mind? School all right?"

"Uh-huh. School's great—I've always liked school. I kind of … you know … miss it. Break and all." Her fingers played lightly with her shirt collar. "No, I wanted to talk to you about something. But … well …"

"No problem. Just start at the beginning or the middle or whatever's easiest." I sat back against the sofa cushions.

"Okay. I kind of rehearsed what I was gonna say but it's escaped me. Let me think. … You were so kind to write that letter for me—you know, the one so I could go on that study abroad program next year."

"Oh, right! The letter. I really love doing that—getting kids out of town and off to another country. I've seen them go, and they always come back so excited after seeing another culture. It makes a change, and I could see you loving that."

She lapsed into silence for several seconds, then said, "Well, that's the thing, you know. I'm … well … I'm not sure that will happen …

now." She glanced down at her hands, folded in her lap. "I'm so sorry that you went to all that trouble."

"No trouble. So why won't it happen? Have you changed your mind?" Silence. She sat stiffly with her fingers nervously intertwining and then opening again. "If your parents aren't sure this is a good idea, I could talk to them, you know."

"No, that's not it."

I tried a different tack. I felt like I was playing twenty questions. "Are your parents moving again? You only just got here, and I thought maybe you'd finish your … your last two years."

"No." She took in a breath. I waited. It seemed like minutes, but it was more like a few seconds. "No, we're staying here. I think. That isn't it." She rubbed her hands together slightly. "I'm just not sure how to say this. Well … ah … I'm … I'm pregnant!" She began crying.

"You're kidding!" I shook my head and then seeing her wide-eyed expression, I backtracked with, "Oh, gosh, I didn't mean to say that. It just slipped out. What a stupid thing for me to say. I'm sorry." I put my arms around her and hugged her tight, feeling her shoulders shaking, and then held her at arm's length. "Stay here; I'll be right back." I headed to the kitchen for a box of tissues. Then, dropping the box on the coffee table, I offered her a handful, and sat down, waiting for the tears to slow down. "I guess I'm just … surprised."

"Yeah, me, too," she sobbed. "More like shocked."

I nodded. "Well, yes. That, too."

"My parents—they'll … they'll kill me, and I don't know what to do. I … I … can't tell them. Oh, God, they're gonna to be so angry."

I stopped to consider how to best approach this. "Well, wait a minute. Wait. Let's back up a bit. Let's think about this. First, how do you know? That is, how do you know you're pregnant?"

"I missed a period."

I looked into her red eyes. "Only one? I'm not sure that means you're pregnant."

"No, it's true. After waiting a while I thought I was just late and … well … I decided I'd go to a doctor. I was really anxious and maybe that was why. I mean, why I missed it. One of my friends—Emily—gave me a name in Peoria. You know, I couldn't go to my doctor here. I just went there with her and the results are back. I was … it was positive," She began sobbing quietly again.

"Oh." I waited a bit. "So is the father around?"

"Around? Well, no. Kevin is in Utah." She scrunched up the tissue into a tiny ball and grabbed another one. "Oh, Mrs. Van Kirk, my parents hate him. I had to leave—no, I was forced to leave him—back home. And every day we've been writing and calling each other. *Every day.*" Her breathing was a little slower now, and she seemed to be more rational. Then her eyes narrowed and she blurted out, "But my parents think he isn't any good. They hate him. They were relieved when my dad got a job here, you know, so far away."

"Hmm." I wasn't quite sure how to phrase my thoughts. "So, if he's there and you're here, how did this happen?"

"I went home—you know, to Utah—to visit some friends. Middle of October, we had a long weekend. I guess that's when. Once. I swear. I swear. We only did it once."

"You know, you're so smart. Did you think about using some protection?"

"I know, I know. But I never thought it would happen the first time." She sniffled. "I haven't told him about … about the baby. I guess it's hard to say that. 'The baby.'" Another balled-up tissue; another new one grabbed. "Well, my parents don't know either. Just you. Now. And Emily." She gave a long sigh and sat back on the cushions. The tears were slowing down.

"Oh, dear. And you've been keeping this inside for how long?"

"Since the beginning of the month."

"A long time to be alone with this."

She used a tissue to dab at her right eye. "I didn't know what to do or who to trust. You know—small school and all. But it just seemed like you would understand. And, actually, I could see you've probably had enough ... I mean, it seemed like it lately ... you know, problems of your own. I mean, sometimes it's easier to understand people with problems if you've dealt with your own ... problems."

I nodded slowly. She was so right. I hadn't had much time to think lately. "This is a pretty complicated situation. You have a lot to decide, even after you do tell your parents—which, by the way, you're going to have to do." She started to protest, and I urged, "I know, I know. You don't want to. Have you given any thought to what you want to do? With the baby?"

Quickly her words tumbled out. "Oh, I can't get rid of it."

I sat back and considered very carefully what I should say. I knew what I'd say to my own daughter, but this wasn't my daughter, and it wasn't my job to tell her what to do. It seemed to me that she would need to tell her parents soon. How could I bring her around to that?

"Then that's one possibility decided—no abortion." I weighed my words. "And what about Kevin? Got any idea how he'll feel?"

"No."

"How old is Kevin?"

"Oh, he's my age. Sixteen, almost seventeen."

In my mind I was thinking about how awful this would be for both their futures, but especially for Wendy's. I didn't know about Kevin, but Wendy was definitely college material. Sixteen years old and pregnant. So many times—for girls—I saw lives changed, college scholarships forfeited, future professions gone before they'd barely been imagined. And at least an equal number of times, I'd seen teenage fathers disappear into another life, leaving any responsibilities for babies behind. It was a sad but true scenario, repeated ad infinitum. This wasn't the first time a student in my class had become pregnant, but no one else had ended up, physically, on my doorstep.

"You have other options like adoption."

"My dad will kill me. He'll snap. You know, he's really involved in our church. Goes every Sunday, Sunday nights, sometimes even goes and helps out with things on Saturdays. It's really conservative. Like him. He'll be so ashamed. He's never liked Kevin, and I can hear him now, hear what he'll say. Oh, man, he'll be so angry. I just can't … I just can't tell him. Just can't …" Her voice trailed off.

"What about your mother?"

Her eyes moved downward and she shook her head back and forth. "She's not gonna be happy either. She didn't like Kevin. She doesn't think he has much future. He never did very well in school like I did." She sighed. "He's not very motivated when it comes to books."

I cleared my throat. "So tell me about him."

"Well, let me think where to start. We got together a year ago. This will be our one-year anniversary next Tuesday." She smiled. "He's wonderful. And he treats me really well. Oh, and he's gorgeous. He has blond hair and the bluest eyes you've ever seen. And sometimes, even though his friends want him to go out with them, he says he'll go with me instead." She grimaced. "My parents, they just don't give him a chance. He works on cars and can do anything like that. He's really good at fixing stuff, and he likes to mess with all kinds of things—you know, engines and radios—things that have to be broken down and put back together. He wants to have his own place some day." She looked down at her hands for a moment and then back up. "Oh, and most important"—and now she smiled broadly for the first time— "we love each other."

At that declaration, one I'd heard so many times—from different boys and girls—I kept my face neutral. What was this? Was I becoming cynical in my middle age? Well, yes, I guess I was.

"All right, then. He sounds like a wonderful guy, Wendy." I calculated my words carefully. "But unfortunately, you can't get along on love these days, especially if you have a baby, which takes us back … have you thought about adoption?"

Her eyes started tearing up again, and she softly shook her head.

"Well, let's get back to your parents. Whatever you do, you'll need to tell your parents first."

"I could never do that," she insisted.

"Oh, Wendy, you have very little choice here. No matter what you decide about the baby, your parents are going to have to be involved."

"But I can't. I just can't. You don't know my parents. They'll kill me."

"Well, I highly doubt that. However, the worst will be over in a few minutes if they do." I smiled slightly. "And if they don't, well, the same is true. How long can they be angry?"

"My *dad? Forever!*" A vehement tone led to an angry set to her lips.

"Start with your mom, then."

She blew her red nose. "I just can't. She'll be so disappointed."

I took a deep breath and put my hand over hers. "Well, I've been around a while. I've seen babies that were unplanned. Lives that were changed. Funny thing about parents and disappointment—after the initial anger or shouting or whatever, they generally calm down and start thinking about what they can do. Even if they're upset, they eventually remember they love you. It's surprising how supportive parents can be once they're over the fireworks."

Out of the corner of my eye I saw Jennifer sidle into the room from around the edge of the dining room wall.

"Mommy, when we go to the library, can we see if Amy wants to go too?"

I smiled at her and said, "Of course we can. You see if you can find your books and put them in a pile on the dining room table." And she was off to the toy room to look for books. I turned back to Wendy and noticed her tears were gone, and she looked preoccupied.

"I suppose he can't stay mad forever," she concluded.

"And maybe your mom could be a co-conspirator, so get her on your side. She might be able to work on your dad. Consider telling her first." And now she was looking calmer and the tears were abating. She was thinking.

"If you'd like, I would be willing to come with you to talk to your parents. If it helps, I could do that. And I don't think your dad will want a witness to your murder."

"No," she murmured. "That's all right. I did this stupid thing—man, really stupid—and now I'll have to see if I can figure out what to say."

"Well, pick a good time. And think about what you're going to say before you start."

She seemed to consider this, her eyes looking out the window behind us. "My little brother has a basketball game this afternoon. Maybe after that."

"Good. ... Think it would help to talk with your mom first?"

"Yeah. I think she can help with my father. Now that I've told you and said it out loud, it seems like I could say it to them. Maybe. Saying it out loud takes some of the anxiety away. But it's going to be awful."

"Well, no matter what, you'll still have a long life ahead of you, whether it's with Kevin or without. I'd put money on your parents helping you think this through."

And now she seemed tired and was winding down. "It just seems like the future is so way out there. You know? I can't imagine."

I smiled. "I understand. You're sixteen and a mom. It's hard to picture—both now *and* down the road—and you'll need to get medical help, prenatal care, to make sure your baby stays in good shape." I took her hand and squeezed it. "So we're agreed. Your parents need to know. Now, let's figure out some opening lines and what comes next. It'll give you courage to have some idea how to start, and where it goes after that will be up to them."

She looked at me and nodded.

By Monday morning I'd not heard a word from Wendy. The phone didn't ring, no one pushed my doorbell, and I hadn't heard of any murders on the local news. So I figured she was now working with her parents to decide what to do.

I sat at my kitchen table and glanced at the clock. 6:30 a.m. The children weren't up yet, and I had some moments of quiet. I put both hands around my coffee cup, hoping to warm them up a bit. As usual, I'd had a terrible night, tossing and turning, thinking things through in my head, and getting used to the nightlight. I had installed a small one in my bedroom last week because I wanted to know which kid was coming in during the night with a nightmare or a request to snuggle up in my bed. Now, I barely glanced at the headlines on the front page of the newspaper that I'd retrieved from the bushes outside the front door. I sighed, thinking about the message of the bathroom scales before I came downstairs. Ten pounds had disappeared somewhere in recent weeks, weight I could ill afford to lose. Then, I heard stirring upstairs, small feet padding across the floor, and I realized the quiet was over, and it was time to think about breakfast.

By eleven, the comforting aroma of hamburger, onion, and taco sauce filled the house, and lunch was simmering on the stove. It was time to start chopping lettuce to make tacos. I could hear Steve playing with building blocks in the toy room. Jennifer was in a chair in the family room, reading a library book and Mike's music was pounding through the floor from upstairs.

Then the doorbell rang.

I ran some water over my hands, loosening bits of lettuce, dried them, and walked quickly to the living room. Maybe it was Wendy, back once again.

Opening the door, I was surprised to see another of my high school students. "Hi, Autumn."

"Hi, Mrs. Van Kirk," she said. I waited. She waited.

Then I broke the silence by asking a question. "What can I do for you? I was actually just about to fix some lunch."

She looked at me with her dark eyes and after a few seconds said, "I was just walking. I do that—walk around, you know. And then I remembered you lived over here. So I looked up your address in the phone book."

"It's nice to see you, Autumn. Is there something I can do?"

"Ah, I don't exactly know. Can I come in?"

I hesitated. "Well … sure. I was just fixing tacos. Would you like to stay for lunch?"

She considered the idea for a few beats. "That would be a good thing, I think."

I took her coat, hanging it in the coat closet, while she pulled back her heavy black hair and straightened her brown sweater. As she was taking off her boots, I went through a list of things I knew about Autumn Swan: Released from a locked mental facility, Autumn had arrived two months ago and been placed in my American lit class. I think she was living with some foster parents. The school nurse had apprised me of all this but not much more, and I occasionally saw her walking down the hall at school, usually by herself. The other kids gave her a wide berth, and I could see why—I felt sorry for her, but she was a little spooky. Her social skills were strange, and she often said things that didn't make sense in the context of the situation. Having her in for lunch made me a bit nervous, but I figured I had a little experience with whatever her problems were. When I was in college I had worked at Research Hospital one summer, a mental facility in Galesburg. I was an aide on various floors, and one of the areas I occasionally worked was the juvenile ward. So I was aware that teenagers in such facilities had various problems, some of them less serious than others. And the hospital had released her. I figured we'd have lunch and I'd send her on her way. Now her boots were off and she was smoothing down a corduroy skirt. My other students wore jeans or sweats on winter weekends.

I said, "Just getting started. Would you like to come out and help me in the kitchen?"

"Sure," she said, looking around at my living room. "Show me what to do and I'll help. Do you have kids?"

"Yes, three," I said as she followed me to the kitchen. "They're all home, and that's why I'm making so much food." I glanced at the pan on the stove, gently bubbling, whetting my appetite with the aroma of tomato sauce, various spices, and onions. It could be spread to accommodate one more person, even though her presence had somewhat dampened my imagined enjoyment of a lazy winter-break meal with my kids.

"Here, you put these plates on the table, and the silverware is in that drawer." I finished cutting the lettuce as she followed my directions, and soon we were ready to load up tacos. I called my three children and introduced them to Autumn, and then silence reigned as we all started eating.

After lunch she stayed and played with Steve, helping him build all kinds of towers with his blocks before they knocked them over. I could hear uproarious laughter as blocks came crashing down. I was at a loss to know what to say, and as the afternoon wore on, she was still here. Finally, I thought I'd try to figure out what was going through her head. I walked into the toy room just as they knocked over the multiple towers with a huge clatter and shrieked uncontrollably.

I'd have to make up something. "Autumn, I'm going to take the kids over to Galesburg pretty soon. Anything you need? Because we're going to be leaving, so it's probably time for you to head back home. I can give you a ride."

"Oh." She seemed a little disoriented as she looked up at me from the floor.

"It's pretty cold out, and it wouldn't be any trouble to drop you at your family's."

"Uh …" Her eyes looked at me and then moved restlessly around the toy room. "Could we talk about that?"

"About what?"

She stood up, brushed off her skirt, and mumbled, "I don't want to go there."

I wasn't quite sure I understood what she'd said, and I answered, "What?"

"Can't I stay here a while longer?"

"Actually, I don't think so. That's why I thought it would be a good idea to give you a ride. It's pretty cold out."

She looked all around the room, then past me, and finally focused in on me once again. "Can we talk about this somewhere?"

"Sure. Why don't we go out to the living room? Steve's got plenty of blocks to pick up and put in their box." I said the last phrase loudly and slowly.

I turned and walked out through the kitchen to the living room, and Autumn followed me silently. Gesturing at the sofa, I sat down and pushed some cushions back to make room for both of us. This seemed to be turning into a psychiatrist's couch.

"So, what's up?"

"Up?"

"Yes. What's the story on not wanting to go home? Can you talk to me about it?"

"Well, yeah. That's … that's why I came over to see you." She licked her dry lips. Then she looked at me. "You seemed like a good person to talk to. It's … you just seem to be so sad sometimes when I see you at school. And then you talk so emotionally when we mention a piece of writing that's … well … sad. I'm sad, too. A lot. So I thought maybe you'd understand. About me, I mean. It's sad but it's also kind of scary."

"All right, I'm a bit confused, so let me try to get this straight. Something is going on at home that has you wanting to be any place but home, right?"

"Yeah. Uh … I'm not sure how to describe it."

"Well, let's start with your home. Don't you live with foster parents?" I smiled, trying to encourage her to explain. Again she licked her lips, and her eyes moved around the room, focusing anywhere but on me.

"I … I live a few blocks from here toward town. My foster parents took me in when I came back here from … from a hospital. My foster mom is okay." She looked down at her hands in her lap. "But my foster father …" And here she stopped a moment and looked up, took a deep breath, and swallowed. Then she looked down again and said very quickly, "My … my foster father … well, my foster father … he comes into my bedroom at night and wants me to do … um … scary things. He gets in my bed and he takes off my pajamas and touches me and has me touch him, and then we have sex, and it hurts me, but I try not to cry, and he says if I tell my foster mom she won't believe me, and then he says that he will hurt me real bad." Her eyes dropped and she sniffled twice, and then there was silence. She looked at her hands.

I think my mouth must have dropped open; I quickly tried to cover my shock. "Autumn, look at me, please. You're sure about this? You wouldn't make something like this up because you don't want to be there, would you?"

"Oh, no, Mrs. Van Kirk. I hate him!" Her hands shook, and her eyes got wider and wider. "He scares me, and I don't want him to hurt me again."

"Has this happened once? Twice? How often?"

"Last night was the last time, but he has come in before on a lot of nights. You see, my mom … er … my foster mother … works at night, and she gets home really late. I'm afraid. I turn my light off and act like I'm really tired and need to get some sleep, but that doesn't stop him at all. Some nights I lie there in the dark, and it's really quiet, and I wait for his footsteps on the stairs and pray that they go past my room. It … my room doesn't lock. I've wanted to tell my foster mom, but I'm afraid he'll hurt me." She looked at me, and I didn't have an idea of what to say. I needed a few moments to get my composure back and consider what to do.

"All right. Stay right here. I'm just going to go check and see what Steve's doing." I searched for something, anything, to stay calm and deal with my shock. "How about a glass of water?"

"Sure."

I walked out to the kitchen. I just needed a few moments to think and get myself together. If this were true—this sexual assault—I needed to get help for her. But, on the other hand, she was just in a mental hospital. If this were a figment of her imagination, a complete fabrication, she could end up hurting the reputation of a totally innocent man. I didn't know this guy. She could be a really good actress, but the fear in her voice seemed real.

I looked in on Steve, who was ignoring the blocks all over the floor and lying on his stomach with a book in front of him. Then another thought occurred to me. Illinois law says any teacher who suspects sexual abuse or assault must turn in the abuser. Every teacher was aware of this law. But in this case, I really wasn't sure if Autumn was telling the truth. I walked back out to the living room. She watched me as I sat down. I asked, "If I get help for this, Autumn, it's very likely you'll be placed somewhere else, away from here. Is this what you want?"

She looked down at her hands, folding and unfolding on her lap. "I don't know. But I don't want to go back there. I just can't go back there."

"All right. I'm going to call the principal from the school. I need to make sure he's aware of this and clear about the situation. He won't tell your parents. Is that okay?"

"Yes" came her quiet, lifeless answer.

I walked out to the kitchen and pulled out a glass from one of the cupboards. Opening the freezer, I filled the glass with some crushed ice. Then I closed the door and walked over to the sink, filling the glass with water. I took it back out to the living room and handed it to Autumn. "Here," I said. "Maybe this will help a little while I see if I can find Mr. Farwell." I pushed the button on the radio, put it on an FM station, and turned up the volume slightly.

I walked back to the kitchen, where I called the principal. He answered on the first ring. I had bought a phone cord that was extra long so I could talk while I was across the room at the stove. After describing Autumn's story, I pulled the long cord after me into the family room and said very quietly, "You remember, this is a student who has recently been in a mental hospital. I don't really know for sure if this is real."

"Well, Sue," he said after a moment, "let me do some checking on this. If I can reach the superintendent, I'll call you back. You're at home, right?"

"Yes." I gave him my phone number, hung up the phone, and went back to talk to Autumn and wait for his call. It came within ten minutes.

"Sue, I spoke with Dr. Jenkins. He called over to DCFS in Galesburg, and they'll take the girl if you want to drive her over. You're covered by the district's insurance, and he says this is the best course of action."

"Even if we aren't sure?" I tried to say it as vaguely as I could in case Autumn could hear me.

"Well, you're right about what the law says. If you even suspect it, you have to turn it in. And in this case it's pretty definite that she doesn't want to be in that house and ... well, being there—you know, physically being there—could put her in jeopardy, so this is our only choice."

Fifteen minutes later, after looking up the location for the Department of Children and Family Services (DCFS) and asking a neighbor to watch my kids, Autumn and I were on our way to Galesburg. I felt anxious about driving her over there, and we were silent most of the way. Autumn had agreed to go with just her purse and coat—I wasn't going to take her to her foster home to collect anything. I anxiously peered out the windows, watching the traffic and considering what I was doing.

Autumn stared out her side window at the snow. The tall black trees along the side of the road seemed thin and vulnerable without their lush green leaves. What a dreary time of year; it was well before the advent of another spring.

Buildings and houses began to appear as we reached the outskirts of Galesburg, and as I drove around the square and up Main Street, I easily found the brick office with its official sign, Department of Children and Family Services. "So this is where the superintendent said I should bring you," I told Autumn. "I'm guessing you've been here before. This okay?"

She looked at me and mumbled, "Yes." Then she grabbed my mittened hand and said, "Thank you. I am so relieved that I don't have to go back to that house again."

I searched her face. Then I smiled. "All right. Let's go and see what we need to do."

We walked over to the office, and an efficient-looking, plump lady at the desk glanced up at us over the rims of her reading glasses. "Is this Autumn?"

"Yes," Autumn said, her voice barely audible.

The lady grabbed a pile of papers. "Come with me."

I started to follow Autumn through a little swinging gate next to the desk but was stopped cold.

"No, just Autumn. You can wait here."

"Sure." I looked around and found a wooden chair near the door. Sitting down, I put my purse on my lap and resigned myself to the possibility that I would have to sign papers or talk to someone about Autumn's situation.

About ten minutes later the woman came back and said, "Everything's fine. You can go."

"But is Autumn—"

"We'll take it from here. Thanks for bringing her in."

I drove the fifteen miles home, relieved of my burden, but I wondered what kind of life this girl would have. Would she, like so many others, be swallowed up and shunted from one foster home to another, as she had been already? I told myself that I had done what I could. Wearily, I drove into my driveway.

The following morning, I was perched in my usual spot in my kitchen, drinking coffee as dawn became brighter outside the windows. Open on the table was a handwritten invitation to a wedding on the weekend. It had arrived in yesterday's mail and I had read it and dropped it on the table. The wedding would be in a private home and would legally bind Wendy Stowe and Kevin Andrews in holy wedlock. "I guess this means they found a way to solve the problem," I said to myself.

I walked over to the dining room and looked out the window at the melting snow. I hadn't heard a thing about Autumn since I'd dropped her off at DCFS. I had called the principal when I returned from Galesburg and told him she'd been delivered. It sounded like I was hauling freight.

Two students, both of them leaving my life—one to enter an uncertain marriage and one to enter yet another uncertain home. And then there was me.

I turned and padded back to the kitchen in my stocking feet, poured more coffee, and sat down once again. I began thinking about how this

Christmas break had gone. I'd never personally dealt with these kinds of horrendous problems. It was easy to teach English, work with students, and not know what was going on in their homes. Sometimes they talked about their home lives or wrote about their problems, but in this case, both girls had somehow found their way to my doorstep. These "home visits" had never happened before, but now they had occurred twice in just a few days.

Maybe they saw me as a kindred spirit, an adult who was open to the sadness. In recent months going to work every day had provided relief, but my students had silently watched as I lost weight, seemed preoccupied, and struggled through the semester. After months and months of wrangling, hassles, and phone calls, struggling to keep my own children safe and stable in a neighborhood and school where they'd feel comfortable, pounds seemed to slide off with no effort. Going to work had been a tremendous relief because it took my mind off my own difficulties. The holidays had seemed rather bleak, and when Wendy and Autumn showed up, their visits just added to the grayness.

I loved my work and students. But I had to guard myself from feeling their sadness so deeply—therein lies too much darkness. I knew there would be better days—for Wendy, Autumn, and me. As Emily Dickinson wrote, "Hope is the thing with feathers/ That perches in the soul." Taking another swallow of lukewarm coffee, I mulled over our three lives, bound together in this piece of time. Then, focusing on my own life, I promised once again to keep myself together—as well as I could—so that my kids' lives would remain on a level track. School and taking care of them—these were the melodies of my current life. I looked up at the calendar on the bulletin board across from me: December 28. Today was the official date that ended my seventeen-year marriage.

Chapter Eleven

Mr. Detroit

Open the 1990 yearbook. Browse through the sports photos. There, that guy. He was All-Conference and Best Offensive football player his senior year. Now, move on to winter sports. He played basketball too. Shift over to spring. He sprinted to first place at Macomb, and he placed third in the entire state in the four-hundred-yard dash. Wander over to the more academic sections. There—see him? He was in National Honor Society, Top Ten, Illinois State Scholar. Perhaps you don't realize he had full-ride scholarship offers from lots of colleges and universities, including most of the Ivy League schools.

Corey Wheeler

Now, thumb through the pages to the senior class photos—he should be there between Teresa Welch and DeeDee Widener. Wait—where's his senior picture? It's missing. Why? The answer to that question is very, very complicated.

Corey Dwight Wheeler spent four years in my life. Our relationship resembled beginning dancers—awkward steps, hesitant understandings of which hand to hold where, and occasional missteps that resulted in explosions. He always told me, "You just don't get it." But now, looking back from the perspective of twenty years, perhaps I did—some of it. Maybe.

By the time Corey Wheeler was in my American lit class during his junior year, I'd come to know his boundaries. You could rummage through a few matters, but you had to tread lightly around others. By junior year he had accumulated lots of A's, sports trophies, and sports records, but I always saw him trudging along as a solitary figure. I'd be on lunch duty near the gym, and he'd come loping down the hallway, hat in his hand, utterly alone. Sometimes he'd stop, and we'd talk. One day I asked him about his family, a subject I knew little about.

"My family?"

"Yeah. I know you have brothers."

"Well, one biological brother and two stepbrothers, but we've been together since I was really young. More like brothers." He said it with an easy smile on his face. He sat on the steps to the auditorium while I sat in a desk nearby. He didn't often smile.

"And you came here from Detroit?"

"Not exactly. Detroit by way of Unity and Macomb."

"Unity?"

"Well," he said slowly, his voice lowering its pitch, "I grew up in Detroit. But we left when I was seven." He glanced down the hallway, scanning the faces.

"I think you told me something about that. Violence?"

"Oh, yeah. I was seeing people get shot and killed right there on the street. Drugs. Blood. Shooting. Everywhere you turned. Those days I had to walk to school. And as a kindergartner, along the way, every so often somebody would just try me … I'm with a kid walking, a couple of kindergartners, and every so often some hulk of a kid would try to step up and test me out. He'd see if I wanna fight. I remember a fifth-grader once decided he wanted to test me right there on the playground." Corey looked toward me but not exactly at me. "So, sure, I was terrified. And my older brother was there, but he didn't step in 'cause he wanted me to fight for myself. So here I was in kindergarten, fighting this gigantic kid, and I'd rip him to shreds. There always was this fighter in me. But you know, everybody in Detroit grew up as fighters, and you'd get beat up at school all the time. That toughness kind of settled into me, seeped into my thinking."

"You're a big talker, Corey Wheeler."

"Honest to God, it's the God's truth. Detroit was an unqualified education."

I thought about that. I, too, had walked to school in first grade, but my biggest obstacle was a growling dog two blocks onto Seminary Street. I looked at this student leaning back on the steps, totally relaxed—a highly unusual state for Corey Wheeler.

"So what about your folks? Did they move you from Detroit to Macomb?"

He peered down the hallway. "Not exactly. My biological dad left when I was six months old. Don't think he'll be around down the road. My mom met my stepdad in a little place in southern Illinois called Tamms. My great-great-grandparents lived there." The corners of his mouth almost smiled. "We stayed with my uncle then. Once my mom remarried, we went to another small town nearby called Unity. You think Monmouth's small? Try a hundred people. Pigs and goats roaming the streets. Talk about a culture shock after Detroit! That's why I laughed when we were reading *Huck Finn*, and he talked about the river towns. That could be Unity. But, you know—the fighting didn't stop even then. Kids still heard 'Detroit' and wanted to call me out. So I was always looking around, looking through the corners of my eyes, ya know? Got to know who's there. Where were they positioned? Who was walkin' behind me?" He pulled his battered hat a little lower over his eyes, which seemed perpetually hooded.

"I suppose if I got in a fight you'd be a good person to have on my side."

He smiled his lazy smile—quite a change from the first time we'd met two years earlier and discussed his class placement …

"Corey, we're just trying to do what's best for you."

He glared at me and put his head back down, a pose he held for several minutes.

"Mrs. Willhardt teaches freshman honors English class. We both think that'd be better for you. You'd be absolutely bored silly in a regular section of English."

He raised his head slightly from the desk. "And you know that because …?" His sullen voice said he was having none of this moving him from one class to another.

I looked at this kid. He was African American, very slender in build, with defined, muscular shoulders and arms, and short-cropped hair. He wasn't a big guy, but he was a powerful guy, and I could almost feel those muscles tightly coiled. His face wore a scowl, and his eyes stayed down on the desk. He had a way of looking continually dismayed. Jan Willhardt and I had already been going at this for fifteen minutes.

"Corey," Jan began once again, "I understand that you might want an easy A, but you really need to be in the honors class. Your test scores show that you could probably get a top scholarship to a college. But you need to have hard classes that will prod you—a grade transcript that shows you've taken those classes."

Silence.

"Corey, Mrs. Willhardt and I have seen hundreds of students go through this high school, and we know real potential when we see it. You're going to have over-the-top college board scores. And from what I hear of your athletic ability, you'll probably get all kinds of offers from big schools. Don't you want that?"

He looked at me with a scornful blast of raised eyebrows and his lips curled back. He let his breath out slowly. No answer. Then, "Look. I don't know why I have to do what you want. I just wanna be in a regular class. No problem. I'm a regular guy. Why can't you just leave me alone?"

"All right," Jan said, "as long as you're in my regular class, I'll just have you do some enrichment work if you won't switch classes."

"That's not fair," grumbled Corey, his shoulders shrugging down deep into his jacket. "I should be able to take the class I want and do what everyone else does."

"But you're not like everyone else," I said. It was time for the big guns. "If you stay in a regular section with Mrs. Willhardt, I'll make sure your grade will be an F." (I couldn't really do this, but it sounded pretty convincing.)

His eyes stared straight out the window, and his mouth was set in a grimace. The sideward tilt of his head showed his anger. I was a little nervous because I didn't really know him and he seemed awfully angry, but I was at the end of my arguments, so it was time to just let it go.

And then, abruptly, he pulled himself out of the desk with an unimaginable grace. "Great! Fine! Do whatever you want with my schedule! You're going to anyway. I don't get anything to say about it!" He grabbed his books and his beat-up hat and went swiftly out of my room.

Only later—many years later—did Corey tell me about his thoughts during this time in his life.

I had seen his grade transcript, and his test scores soared into the miraculous regions of chartland. And I'd heard from track devotees around school that he was Mercury when it came to running. But he didn't want to be pushed, didn't want to be challenged. As it turned out, despite his reluctance to enter the honors program during his freshman year, he did well with Jan Willhardt's honors English class, and then he moved on to me.

He wrote a paper that year about football. I watched football and knew the basic ebb and flow of a game, but I'd never been there—not on the field, not getting the bone-jarring, crunching, air-exploding-from-the lungs flavor of what it was really like. Corey spelled it out in this paper, along with every ferocious hit and why he loved it.

"And this is really why you play football?"

"Oh, yeah." He smiled. "Sometimes I have so much anger with nowhere to go. Don't know what to do with it. Don't know where it comes from, but I know when I go out there on that field that I can let it go; kind of use it to my advantage, and it's the place to do that. It's legal. It allows me to ... well, kind of to express myself. An outlet, I guess."

I was horrified. "You think it's okay to hurt people?"

"Oh, that's just the breaks of the game, you know. It's like ... I don't know ... like maybe a badge of honor. You send a guy on the other team to the hospital, and that's how you play the game. That's one less bozo you need to handle, and the other guys understand not to mess with you. Feels good."

"And that doesn't bother you at all?"

"Bother me? I remember a game where I broke a kid's arm. Heard it crack. And I looked down on him, and I didn't feel nothing. No mercy. I know that's hard for you to get and all, but I can't do that anywhere else. The football field. Rage. Get it out there."

"But where does it come from? Why are you so angry at everything?"

"If I could figure that out, that'd be something, wouldn't it? But man, do I love that game because it works for me. And people look up to me 'cause I can do that. They're always talkin' to me about the game coming up, sometimes the one before. People I don't even know stop me."

Some of his words made sense to me. He set records in football, carrying the ball and racking up press releases and honors. I thought about the set of his eyes, the passion in his voice. That was a place he felt he belonged—familiar territory, with rules and understandings and ways you related to people. But putting kids in the hospital? I shook my head. I'd never understand that.

Later that year the honors classes went on an annual field trip to Circa '21, a dinner theatre in the Quad Cities. Because I had to be home at an earlier time than the others, I drove myself rather than travel with the classes. Corey asked if he could ride along with me. That day, he was in a somber, more meditative mood, but he was talking. I'd often found a car ride was a great way to talk to my own children, especially about tough topics, because they didn't have to look at me, and they couldn't get out while the car was moving.

I searched for a topic. "So, have a date to prom?"

"Nope."

I waited a few seconds. Then, "How come?"

He looked out the window. "Nobody to ask."

"Ah, come on. There are plenty of girls out there who would love to go with you."

"Not really." He was silent for several seconds and then quietly said, "You don't get it."

"Okay, so explain. Don't clam up. How about explaining to me whatever it is that I don't get?"

He was quiet for a minute or two. When he spoke, his voice stayed soft, at least for awhile. "You don't get it, Mrs. Van Kirk. And that's okay. You're not like me. You know?" I kept my eyes on the road but I could sense the tension in his voice. He hesitated; I assumed he was trying to figure out how to phrase his words or maybe whether to say anything. Through the corner of my eye I could see him glancing out of the side window, seeming to make up his mind about it. "You never grew up where I did, never went through what I've been through, and we're not alike in any way. What do you think I do on the weekends? Go out with the guys? Go on dates with girls—and by the way, white girls? Black girls? Tough to find someone in this school who looks like me. My brother dates white girls but I just can't do that—can't do that to fit in. Doesn't work for me.

"And then there's the weekend. Am I celebrating? After the game—am I out celebrating? No! How can I? And you know what the other guys are doing? They're at parties, smoking and drinking and throwing up. That me? Hell, no! Ya see, I see that at home. Alcoholism. Runs in my family. Don't need any of that, and I've sworn I'll never ever take a drink. Never. Seen what it does to my family, and someday I'm gonna be a dad, gonna have kids, and I swear they will never ever see their dad like that. No parties for me. No dates for me. I just go home and close the door to my room and type on the keyboard. That's my life." He spat out those last three words. "They're out celebrating victories that I helped win, and I'm typing away so I don't have to think about other stuff. ... That's why, why you're not like me."

That was more than he'd said to me in two years. And he was right. I wasn't black in a school that was 97 percent white, and I'd never played football, and I hadn't thought about how he might date–or not date. After that outburst, I wasn't sure what to say. "I'm sorry, Corey. You're right. It would be—it is—hard to understand what you're feeling. So …" I tried to think of something to say. "Who do you run around with?"

He blew out a long breath, and I wondered if he thought he'd said too much in this tenuous relationship. Ours was a connection feeling its way, trying to accommodate, to delicately force concessions.

"Good question," he conceded. "It's the box thing."

"The box thing?"

"Yeah. See, I'm all about academics these days. And football. But in school, that won't work for other people. Most of the black kids in school—least the ones I see—aren't there about books. That puts me in a box." He turned his head to the side again and glanced out the window. "They think I'm a nerd cause I get good grades. I'm a 'sell-out.' I just gotta remember they aren't going where I am, so if I'm a sell-out, so be it. It's just a tiny box." And now he sighed. "Then there's the football thing. White people don't get it. They like the fact that I'm an athlete, but they don't get that academic thing. They just like the fact that I'm strong, aggressive, fast on my feet. But go out with their daughters? Get a college scholarship? Not in their picture of me. So that box I'm in gets smaller. There's no one I can go out with and hang out with that will understand me, and vice versa. Then a lot of kids drink and that puts me in an even smaller box because I don't. I know everybody and they know me but hell, there isn't any way they can relate to what I'm going through. And what I don't understand—doesn't make sense—is why the few other black kids at school don't talk about this. They must feel some of what I'm getting."

"Have you tried—really tried—to talk to any of these guys, black or white?"

"Yeah, I know. I keep to myself. But once I get to know people, I talk more. I just never can make any close friends, the kind you tell everything to. No confidants. Only myself. Everything's inside—lots of stuff—but no one to get it out to. No one my age."

"No one?"

"Well, there's a couple of guys that I'd kinda count as friends. Danny Munson, Scott Pieper. They've got no vested interest in hanging out, and they cross a lot of social lines. They're the closest. But again, they don't get it. Not completely."

I was silent. What to say? "Maybe you should just keep your eyes open, find guys who are around you in things you like, and try to approach them about the hanging-out thing."

"Maybe." He was being kind with that answer and could probably sense my indecisiveness. After a few minutes I decided he was right. I didn't know what to say. Maybe try a safer zone.

"Tell me about your computer."

"My computer." His tension shifted into soft laughter. His back and shoulders settled in to the car seat, and his voice slowed down. Safer ground. Then he said, "Got it 'cause I talked my parents into sharing the load."

"Sharing the load?"

"Well, I saw this movie, *2001: A Space Odyssey*. It had a computer, Hal, that was incredibly smart. He could write computer programs that were practically human. Fascinating. And I said to myself, 'If I could do that, man, I could change my world. What a powerful, cool possibility. I think that's it.'"

"What's it?"

"I kinda knew in an instant that was what I'd do with my life. Write programs that could do all those things."

"Could be a plan."

"Yeah." He turned and looked at me, his hands up and moving along with the excited words. "But I didn't have a computer. And where was I gonna get one when I didn't have the money? So I went to my parents. 'Course they said, 'A computer? You're talking two thousand dollars, and where are we gonna get that kind of money?'"

"I'm assuming this is leading to a deal, right?"

"You got it. I said if I could get half that amount, could they pay the rest? And they were thinkin' 'Where are you gonna get a thousand dollars?' I'd work for it. Got a job workin' in a cornfield detasseling corn to get it. Five o'clock in the morning I'm waiting—taking the bus to the field—and I come back every night at six o'clock. Long, sweating, swearing, dog-tired days. I did it most of the summer until the day of my disaster. Forgot to take my hat. It was probably, oh, a hundred degrees in that field. After suffering heat delirium, I started pulling up armfuls of corn by the roots and slinging them all over the place." Suddenly he laughed. "Least that's what they told me. After that I quietly got back on the bus, lay down for a while, and never detasseled another cornstalk again. God, that was a horrendous summer."

"But you got the money?"

"Yeah. Never worked so hard in my life. So I took it to my parents and said, 'Okay, here's my half of the money, and I still wanna buy a computer.' Come Christmastime, my parents had it. I bought a couple of books about programming, and read them, and reread them cover to cover, and probably turned back the corner of every other page. Learned to do some basic programming." He chuckled. "And now I'm so good at it, I'm helping the computer teacher teach it to the other kids."

I didn't know much about computers so I thought I'd keep him talking by asking him about his computer. "So what kind of computer did you buy?"

He laughed—it was a low, he-he kind of noise. "It's a Radio Shack Tandy 1000 EX, complete with an RGB monitor and keyboard. And it has a whopping 256K of memory. Runs at a 4.77/ MHz clock speed."

"A foreign language to me. No wonder I don't understand, according to you."

"Gonna remember those numbers the rest of my life. When I'm not studying or practicing sports, I'm in front of that baby. Friday nights, I just go home from football and write programs and games and try to figure it all out. Not the same as hanging out with people. But that's just not gonna happen. I go out and occasionally walk the strip. Got no place to go and no one to call up. Random motion. And everyone else is at parties. I walk around for a while 'cause I can't sit in front of that computer all the time. But then I realize it's pretty aimless, walkin' around, so I head back home to my room."

"You know that computer might become a college major."

"Maybe. It's kind of fascinating to me—that I can do it. I can make this program from the ground up and make it do what I want it to do."

"At least you have something you're passionate about. Who knows where it might lead? Really!"

He smiled his quiet smile. It made me wonder if he was thinking, *Okay, so you do get that about me, but the rest—no.*

When I thought back to that day, that conversation, what I remembered was how solitary, how sad, how desperately lonely his weekends must have been with just the computer for company.

During his junior year, he was in my American lit class, and he quit the track team for a while. I had heard rumors, whispers, that there were "problems" with him in that sport. So one day I caught up with him in the hallway over the lunch hour and asked him about it. He seemed down that day, despairing.

"I heard a rumor that you weren't running anymore. How come? Did something happen? Someone call you something ugly?"

"Nah." He stayed a few feet away and simply talked toward my general direction. "I'm done, Mrs. Van Kirk. I'm just done. Over. It doesn't do anything for me, and it isn't fun anymore."

"Well, I know it's not like football, but—"

"So true. Nothing like football. I kinda felt pressured into it. I'm the fastest runner in the school." He said it as a fact, not to brag. "People expect me to use that, and they put pressure on me."

"Pressure? Who? Who does that?"

"A lot of adults. Teachers. Parents of kids. Kids. They expect it. 'Come on, Corey, you could really rack up some records. Maybe go to state.' And if that doesn't work, it's 'The team needs you.' It's a lot of pressure. And if I have a bad day, they think I'm not trying very hard, and they say, 'He's just lazy.' You know, even pro athletes have bad days. Too much pressure. Pressure to win. I feel like I'm under a microscope. Newspaper write-ups. Interviews. I wanna to do this for the right reasons, not for everyone else. This town is sports-crazy, and everyone's expectations of me are really high because I'm in three sports. It takes the fun out of playing sports."

"Did you talk to the coach about all this?"

"Yeah. He says the same thing—bad day, not trying. He told me if I didn't enjoy competing anymore, I should quit. So I did."

"But don't you miss it?"

"Nah. Too much pressure. But I feel bad, like I'm letting my teammates down. I just need some time, I guess, to figure it out. It's not like football. Football's about aggression and—"

"Yup, I remember that discussion."

He lowered his head for a minute; then he looked up at me and said, "I got some things to figure out." He turned away and ambled down the hallway toward the office.

He was always alone, I thought, usually home on the weekends or week nights. Now even his sports world—the place where there were definite rules, structure, success—was also tumbling down on him. I needed to do something to help him, but I didn't know what.

Over the next few days I found my mind going back repeatedly to his absurdly difficult position—Corey's situation at this school. I considered how I dealt with race in my classes. When we talked about *Huckleberry Finn*, I explained the history of the word "nigger" and why it was part of that time, of that book. If we read a passage out loud in class, I always made sure that I was the one to read it if it had "that word." I thought I was being sensitive, but perhaps I wasn't. One time, I passed back a paper that had multiple errors throughout, and the kid—a young black student—threw his paper down on his desk and said, "Aw, you just give me that grade because I'm black."

I think I was shocked at first. But then I said, "Check it with the kids on either side of you. Your grade is as objective as theirs. And don't try that on me again." Wasn't it enough to treat students with as much respect as I could muster, no matter whether they were black, white, or gray? Well, not gray, but that would be the point.

Scout, the overly perceptive narrator in *To Kill a Mockingbird*, said, from a later vantage point in life, that she remembered her father, Atticus, saying you could never understand a man until you walked a mile in his shoes. I didn't know how I could possibly do that in the shoes of Corey Wheeler.

Then I remembered Art.

Art Toler was a good friend, an African American kid who was sent to school here, where his grandparents lived, because the schools in DC were too violent. I had taught Art in high school and now he was well out of school, in his twenties, and finishing a degree at Western Illinois University in Macomb. We became friends, and I valued his help at my house. He occasionally stayed for meals, and I felt it was great for my boys to get to know him, a person of great warmth and kindness. In high school he seemed to be accepted by black and white kids alike, and he had a sense of humor that helped that divide. I didn't realize then how many masks he wore.

Of course, I didn't know how he did it—walked that line between races—but somehow he did. In high school he had a signature dance move called the Fish, and the kids all applauded him and cheered on his impromptu performances in the stands at ball games. He seemed to be universally loved. So if anyone could help Corey, it was Art. I didn't want to push or prod Corey, so I'd have to be careful about getting him to meet Art. Corey was clear about making his own decisions, but he'd have to trust me on this one.

Art lived in a small apartment on South First Street near a funeral home called Turnbull's. I talked Corey into stopping over there with me one weekend afternoon. He seemed a bit restless and nervous.

"And we're going to meet this black dude, why?"

"Oh, he's just a friend of mine, and I figured maybe the two of you would have a lot in common. And maybe he'd understand what you keep telling me I don't. He graduated from the high school."

He fell silent and seemed to be digesting that thought. We pulled up in front of Art's place, and Corey followed me into the house. Art had a first floor apartment, where the front door opened into a small, dark living room. He also had a kitchen and a bedroom, each with very high ceilings because it was an old, rambling house that had been subdivided into various apartments. The furniture was bits and pieces of this and that, all looking extremely well worn. After I introduced the two of them, it was awkward at first. After all, I'd put two total strangers in a room and pushed them together like little kids on the playground. But as I watched and listened to the two of them, subtle changes began.

Art Toler had always treated me like a middle-class white woman with three kids who was his high school teacher. We were friends, but when we were together, he talked to me like a grown-up friend, an equal in a white world. And he spoke standard English—my world. But listening to him talk to Corey was an ear-opening, bizarre performance. Art lapsed into an urban black dialect that was wholly unfamiliar to me but totally familiar to Corey. Corey's voice was excited, and the longer they talked, the more his hands gestured. I was used to that with Art—never a dull moment when he was around. But something was happening with Corey—an understanding. A revelation.

As I listened and watched, they talked about topics I knew little about—a new form of music called house music that hit Chicago in the '80s; urban black radio stations in Detroit and DC that were impossible to pick up here unless the atmospheric conditions were perfect; rap music that I had slightly heard of; athletics; pro teams they followed; and finally, Art's experience at the high school and how he understood the feelings of desperation, isolation, and loneliness that Corey was feeling. Art seemed to have it all together now that he was older and could look back on high school. When we got up to leave, he shook Corey's hand and told him to stop by any time. I smiled at Art, and he laughed at me, knowing full well that I had just experienced an alien world. I shook my head but thought that bringing Corey had been the right thing to do. I didn't realize at the time that it would also become the seeds of another incident to fuel Corey's anger.

I lost track of Corey during his senior year. I didn't have him in class anymore and while I talked with him in the hallways, he was on to other things. But he seemed a little more relaxed, a little more balanced. Maybe that came from Art's talk, maybe from being a senior and more mature. I didn't know.

But then came a conversation I didn't want to have with him. I had to find him in the hallway to tell him the worst news: Art was dead—a self-inflicted gunshot wound. No one understood why. There was a great deal of speculation, because he had been on anti-depression medicine, a fact I didn't know. His aunt Carole had stopped by my house to give me the news firsthand. I knew that Art had been living in Macomb, had married, and seemed very much in love and was doing well. Then this.

At school the next day I sought out Corey because I didn't want him to hear this on the news. He was walking down the hall, smiling, a sign that his world was better. But once I stopped him to talk and told him about Art, his eyes clouded over, the stubborn anger appeared around his mouth, and his hands came up.

"I'm sorry, so sorry, Corey. It's a horrible loss. I cared about him so much, and now he's gone and I don't know why."

He looked me in the eye—a gesture that seldom ever happened with him—and he spat out, "I understand exactly why he did it!" And he walked away.

Only years later did I begin to understand the currents that blew through Corey's world in high school, winds that would have a direct influence on his adult world. Computers did become his life and remained a constant through some harrowing turns in the road. The moments when our paths crossed again revealed a Corey who had achieved some success and was more confident. I knew he realized how hard it was for me to understand his teenage life. I had struggled to find the right things to say to him. I would find out years later that only once did I succeed.

He went to Morehouse College, a decision based on very little information. He knew nothing about choosing colleges but wanted to go south, find a large city, and be part of a predominantly black school—total change from Monmouth. He'd had scholarship offers from practically every Ivy League college. Later, he would regret the Morehouse decision, but on one of his unannounced trips back, he stopped in to see me, and I asked him to come talk to my high school classes. I particularly wanted him to address the problem of African American students and studying, because it was "not the thing to do." He had grown up. The anger was gone. He looked people in the eye, and he spoke eloquently about the future of my high school kids—if they studied.

At that point Corey was a sophomore at Morehouse and not particularly fond of the school or its academic program, but he was overjoyed by Spelman, an all-women's college—predominantly black—that was right next door. He was picked up by Exxon for the summer after his freshman year, talking his way into an internship of programming their computer systems. He spent the next two summers doing that and also working for them over Christmas breaks. Computers were paying off for him. Exxon had been reluctant to hire him but discovered he knew too much about computers not to do so. IBM had also approached him to work on their systems, but by then he was content with Exxon in Houston.

When he returned to Morehouse for his junior year, his scholarship was gone, evidently blown away by embezzlement from the endowment fund by some of the college's now-fired administrators. He never finished college. I didn't know that, of course, because I only caught up with him again several years after that.

He was hired in Chicago at the national headquarters of the YMCA. They were working with a computer company called EDS. At first he was a senior computer systems engineer who reviewed network plans. But when it became obvious that his criticisms of the system came into dispute with their engineers, Microsoft was called in and agreed with Corey. He became the lead engineer for the project, staying with the Y for several years.

Today he has a family and owns his own computer consulting firm. From that vantage point, he looks back on his high school years with a wisdom and a quietness only time can offer.

"If I could go back and do high school over, I'd have more fun. Listen to more people. Man, I was nothing but anger back then. Didn't have a senior picture. Maybe you didn't know that. Couldn't stand to look at myself, even in the mirror in the morning. Got dressed in the dark. I was angry about every aspect. Especially how I looked. Not like anyone else in Monmouth.

"I have a bagful of medals from track in high school. I kept every medal, every clipping, even from junior high. They were all scattered around in various drawers. I kept them less for myself and more for my kids. Knew I'd have kids, and maybe one day they'd want to see what kind of athlete their dad was. I was never so proud as I was crossing the finish line in the state track meet. Went to state twice. And to this day

I have never had a drink. I made a promise, and I kept it to this day. Then, of course, there was my dad's leaving us. That experience makes me very close to my kids, and I made that promise, too: I was never going to leave them like he did.

"You know," he chuckled, "I was kinda hard on you back then. You didn't get me, but that was okay 'cause you tried. You and Señora Segura. You were the two. Back in high school, you told me something that I have always held on to for motivation. It was during one of those bleak, crummy days, where I couldn't see anything beyond my anger. It was early days for computers, but you knew how much I held on to mine, like a life raft in the middle of an ocean. You said that people would pay me for what I knew, and the more I knew, the more they would pay me. I chewed on that advice for a couple of years. I knew even then that I was black, living in a white world, and the more I knew, the better I could compete. I'd have to know twice as much as the white guys. The advantage was to educate myself. So I went out and began devouring books. I took that to heart, I told my own kids that, and I took a book to work in my backpack every day when I was working for other people. Knowledge and how you use it—I never put *not* knowing to chance. Even now, I never stop learning. Turns out—about that—you were right."

Chapter Twelve

The Boy Who Dreamed He Could Run

In my first conversation about Brian Hendel, I rarely used his name, but despite his anonymity, I still felt apprehensive.

"He's in a what?" I asked.

"A wheelchair. He's a quadriplegic."

"You have to be kidding!" I burst out. "I'm teaching an English class. How will he write?"

"He'll have an aide with him who'll take notes and probably do the actual writing. He'll simply dictate what he wants to say."

I considered what else I should ask the learning disabilities teacher, Linda Clark. "What else do you know about him?"

"Well, let's see. He has a really first-rate brain and a great sense of humor. He's only going to be in school in the afternoons, and he'll be in your last class of the day with your sophomores. He'll have an aide with him, who might have to aspirate his lungs occasionally if he has breathing problems."

"The aide might have to do what?"

"Well, she might have to suction him and give him oxygen if he starts having breathing problems." Linda saw my despair. "But I'm told this doesn't happen very often. Oh, yes—he's had a tracheotomy to help his breathing so he has this little thing—like a plug put into a hole in his neck—so he can talk. But his aide will be with him and can take care of all that." She frowned slightly. "Don't worry. You'll be fine."

As I listened to Linda, I wondered how this situation would ever work. I had eighteen students in that class. What would they think about this kid in a wheelchair who had all of those problems? What if they said things that hurt his feelings? And how was I going to corral the eighteen of them while also worrying about how to deal with this kid in a wheelchair? No one ever taught me a thing about how to teach English to students who had physical disabilities.

To be fair, I had already had some students with *learning* disabilities. In 1972, the federal government passed the Individuals with Disabilities Act, which assured the rights of disabled individuals in all kinds of situations. I applauded the idea but hadn't been fully faced with its reality. Since that time, all of us teachers had learned—mainly by trial and error—how to teach students who had various learning disabilities. My only brush with a *physically* disabled student was a girl with a hearing impairment. For her, I simply had to make sure that I stayed in front of her and spoke clearly so she could read my lips. This worked well, but I had to think it through ahead of time. When I gave oral vocabulary tests, I had to make sure I didn't move around. Because my own teaching style involved lots of movement up and down rows, I simply changed my habits and didn't have any problem with teaching the whole class.

But a quadriplegic? I'd never even been around someone who didn't have the use of arms or legs. The closest was Uncle Vito, who had polio as a child, which caused him to walk with a cane. Not even close to being quadriplegic.

"Linda, I have to tell you this is making me kind of nervous," I confessed. "Got any suggestions?"

Linda picked up Brian's papers from her desk and handed them to me. "Have a talk with his aide—Jeanie Morrison—and see what she says. She's been with him for a while and can probably give you some help. I know you can work it out, and I think you'll find that this adds a new dimension to your class."

I left the school that day feeling very put upon—"new dimension," indeed. It was enough that I had more than ninety students to deal with during the course of the day. Several had varying learning disabilities, and I had to make sure I changed their quizzes and tests to accommodate their difficulties. I planned activities so that they wouldn't miss anything by leaving class to take their exams in the LD room. LD students added myriad details to the rest of my day, with five classes, one study hall, and three different preparations. I had worked with Linda, and she was an amazing facilitator, but I was still responsible for teaching her students in my classes.

When I began teaching, learning disabilities weren't recognized or understood. As time went by, I learned a great deal—from Linda and from my own reading—about ADHD (attention deficit/hyperactivity disorder) and ADD (attention deficit disorder.) Other than that, there was absolutely no preparation or training. And now I was expected to have a student in a wheelchair who couldn't use his arms or legs. I wasn't sure it was a good idea to mainstream (integrate students with special needs into my regular classroom) these students—not for the "special" students or the rest of the population. But this was the situation, so I would have to try to make the most of it. I decided to start by preparing the rest of the class.

The first day that Brian Hendel came to my class, I had moved the desks near the door so he would have plenty of space. I'd also brought a chair in from the teachers lounge across the hall so his

Brian Hendel

aide could sit with him. That was my entire plan. His caregiver, Jeanie Morrison, a registered nurse, was a diminutive woman with an air of quiet competence. She introduced herself and Brian and sat down next to him after checking to see if he needed anything. I was taking roll, watching my students come in, and confirming that they had their literature books. The bell rang, and I went over to tackle "the new guy."

As I walked over to Brian with his books, I took a second to check him out. He seemed very small compared to my other students, but I realized he'd had muscular dystrophy for a long time. He was wearing a dark sweater and pants that dwarfed tiny legs. He was strapped into his wheelchair, and he seemed to have a brace of some sort that held his body in a sitting position and created shoulders with strange ridges under his sweater. His right hand rested on a small platform, and his thumb was on what looked like a joystick, which evidently controlled the electric chair. His other hand lay lifeless in his lap. Maybe he wasn't completely without the ability to use his hands. He had come in ahead of Jeanie Morrison so, I figured, he must be able to control the chair himself. And yes, he did indeed have some little thing protruding from his neck.

I took a deep breath and digested all of these details rather quickly and nervously, because I was feeling a bit guilty for staring. Then my eyes moved to Brian's face. It was round and had that well-scrubbed look of a baby, with the pale skin tones of a redhead. His hair, cut fairly short and feathered back stylishly, was light brown with reddish tints. Glasses with wide square frames settled on his large and perfectly triangular nose. Heavy eyebrows complemented his hair and skin, and when I looked into his eyes I saw the most unexpected and amazing thing—they seemed to twinkle. He was smiling a huge, broad grin. I couldn't help but smile back.

"Hi, Brian."

"Hi," he responded shyly.

"I'm glad you're here. Everyone has been eagerly awaiting your arrival. We weren't sure whether this was the day, but we've been planning." I smiled, even as I heard myself prattle on about absolutely nothing.

He also smiled, but his was quizzical, as if he weren't sure what to reply, so I hurriedly added, "And I think maybe today we'll just have you listen in, and if you can stay a few minutes after class, we can talk about what I can do to make this work for you. Is that okay?"

He seemed to catch his breath for a moment, then grinned and said yes. Those eyes sparkled and in his reticent single syllable, it seemed like *he* was perfectly at ease with this whole experience. I returned to my desk, feeling guilty and reproaching myself for ever feeling annoyed with this child.

During that first class, my other students occasionally stole furtive glances in Brian's direction. Before Brian came, I had explained to the class that he'd had muscular dystrophy since he was in grade school. They may not have understood what this entailed, and they hadn't asked any questions. If they were curious about Brian's condition, they evidently decided to hold off until they were able to see the new kid themselves.

The class ended, and I moved my desk chair over next to Brian and Jeanie to have a word with them. Mostly, I was interested in their advice. "I know I didn't have you say or do anything today, Brian, but I thought it would be a good first day to just let you get used to the classroom, the other students, and me."

"Yes … that was good," he said slowly, with a long pause in the middle to catch his breath.

"I think this is going to work just fine," Jeanie said, and we talked about some mundane chores, like getting extra textbooks.

Just fine? I reflected in my head. *You have to be kidding. I have no idea how this is going to work.* But I articulated, "If it's all right, Brian, I think I'll just call on you sometimes, but I'm not sure how to know that you want to volunteer an answer."

"I'm … not sure how … you can … do that either," he murmured, placidly breathing between words.

"I'll do some thinking about that." I then directed a question at Jeanie, hoping she would give me some indication of how students were reacting. "Have his other classes gone all right?"

She turned in her chair, looking at Brian. "It's been pretty funny, hasn't it, Brian?" He blinked his eyes, concentrating on her words. "Everyone's been fine, and no one's been mean or said anything they shouldn't. Mostly the kids ignore you because they aren't sure how to act." Then to me: "Occasionally we've had kids in the hallway ask what is 'wrong' with him, and sometimes they act like he can't talk, see, or understand anything. But we're used to that, aren't we, Brian?" she finished reassuringly.

He grinned at her, a secret social club of two.

"How long have you been together?" I asked.

"About three years. He's a great kidder. We laugh a lot."

It occurred to me after they left that I had mostly talked about Brian to Jeanie as if he hadn't been sitting there.

Eventually, I learned to call on Brian Hendel, and I reached a point where I could see by his eyes that he wanted to say something. Then Jeanie would either put the plug in his neck so he could talk or he would have enough air through his nose to breathe.

Occasionally she'd have to take him out of the room to "bag him," a phrase I found repugnant, but which meant that he needed to have phlegm suctioned out of his throat so he could breathe better. My asthmatic self felt uneasy, because the inability to breathe was something I understood, and I felt rather anxious each time Brian was in distress. But frankly, just listening to him struggle for breath occasionally made me very nervous. I knew that feeling of suffocation.

Senior picture, 1992

While I was a teacher who often walked down rows of students and touched a shoulder here, an arm there, if I felt a flinch or a brief pulling back, I knew not to touch that student again. But with Brian, it was different; I didn't get so close. I mulled over my reaction a great deal and, guilt-ridden, tried to make myself accountable. At last, I realized that his breathing made me uneasy, and so I kept my distance.

It seemed strange to have another adult in the classroom. I don't know if it was that anomaly or the chemistry of my students that made this class a smooth experience. And it became a class joke that Brian drove his chair so fast that we were sure he was going to run someone down in the hallway. One day after he left a few minutes early, zipping through the door at the speed of light, Brian Cook said to me, "He is really something, isn't he?"

"Meaning what?" I asked curiously.

"Well," he said. "I mean he's here every day. He never misses. I wonder what it takes to get him dressed and everything so he can get here?"

"That's a good question. Maybe you should ask him."

"Ah, no. I couldn't do that. He'd think I was makin' fun of him."

"He seems to be really smart. How can a kid in a wheelchair like that be so smart?" added Ty, another student sitting near Brian.

"Well," I began, "is his brain affected by sitting in a wheelchair?"

Ty thought about this for a second. "No, I guess that's true. I hadn't thought about that."

"Yeah, he always seems to have the answers when no one else does," said Brian Cook.

"Do you suppose maybe he reads his assignments?" I asked.

Brian sighed. "Probably."

"Maybe the speed demon's teaching you a lot more than I am." And that point wasn't lost on me—the woman who formerly thought mainstreaming disabled students would be a nuisance.

Later that year, Brian experienced a change in caregivers—Jeanie was going to a different job. One day Brian came in with Jeanie and another woman named Kathy Gobbett. Kathy was short and small, with reddish hair. She was very talkative, and she and Brian shared a lot of laughter, just as he had with Jeanie Morrison.

That day we were working in small groups. I often had students working in groups, and sometimes I kind of set up the kids to work with Brian. I'd ask Brandy to make sure Brian got to agree with answers and say the answers in their group, and I'd catch B. J. or Amy in the hallway to tell them Brian was going to be in their discussion group. Would they please make sure they included him in their deliberations? Sometimes this worked pretty well, and sometimes Brian was quiet. I guess he could have a subdued day occasionally if he wanted to.

One day we did a Jeopardy game to review for the Shakespeare test. Brian's group soon became aware that he always knew the answers. They could count on him to know every answer, and he also got them double points on hard questions and knew the "Final Jeopardy" answer—always. He was the hero of the day. Brian seemed to take a perverse pleasure in fooling the group with one idea and then correcting it when they questioned his choice. I watched and listened to him as he did that, and I secretly smiled. He loved to have jokes with them, and it became apparent that they were pretty astounded by his brainpower. After that, everyone wanted him in their groups for anything competitive.

Somewhere during this time I had a parent conference with Brian's parents, Jerry and Kris Hendel. I asked them about the history of Brian's muscular dystrophy because I didn't know anything about his past. Jerry said that Brian had been born with muscular dystrophy and didn't walk until he was eighteen months old; his ability to sit up was also delayed. The Matherville elementary school tested him at age four and said he was "slow."

"We knew for some time that he seemed to be behind the other kids his age, so we took him to Iowa City, and they did a muscle biopsy and confirmed that he had MD," added Kris.

"Could he walk at all then?" I asked.

"Oh, yes," said Jerry. "In fact, he can remember walking. He had leg braces in second and third grade, and some of the janitors at the school made him a 'stander' with a tray on it so he could be upright and have support."

"I see. He was charming the janitors clear back then!"

Kris smiled and said, "Matherville had fabulous teachers. Two of them came in early to do physical therapy with Brian. He's always had a good attitude about the whole thing. Now, don't get me wrong; he isn't a saint. Brian has his days when he doesn't feel like doing something, and we have to get a little stern with him. But mostly, he's managed to keep all of us going."

"How'd you happen to end up here in Monmouth?"

Jerry answered, "Eventually, Brian got to high school in the Matherville district, and the principal and superintendent felt he would be better served at a special school in the Quad Cities."

"But it would be a self-enclosed classroom," Kris added. "We talked it over, and this was a problem for us. He was always happiest when he was with other kids, and being a teenager presented a whole new group of issues. So we decided that we wanted him in mainstreamed classrooms with other teenagers. All Brian wants is to be treated like everyone else."

"So you decided to come here to Monmouth?"

"Yes. We knew, of course, about the private school for disabled kids here in Monmouth, but we wanted to have Brian in public school classrooms as long as we could manage it. Brian also has a four-year-old sister, Lauren, whom we adopted. This has been a wonderful thing, because they get along beautifully, and she worships him as her big brother. He teases her unmercifully."

"That's one thing I've noticed about Brian," I said, "and so do the students—he has a wicked sense of humor."

"And we are so grateful for that," added Jerry.

"How does this affect your days and household? How do you both manage to work and deal with all of this?"

"Well, we have a nurse who brings him to school, as you know, but we get up very early in the morning and get him ready," Kris said. "He has serious digestive problems, so he takes medicine for that, but it also takes him quite a while to eat—his food has to be processed so it's smooth for him to swallow. He goes to school in a van that's made to take his wheelchair, and he's only here in the afternoons. Then Jerry and the evening nurse help him with his homework. And we have Lauren to watch and take care of too. So, yes, it is a twenty-four-hour-a-day job. And nothing is fast. It takes quite a while to get him ready for school and feed and bathe him, and then in the evenings it takes a lot of patience to help him with homework. But we manage." Kris looked at her husband, who nodded.

After the Hendels left, it occurred to me that I didn't ask a thing about Brian's future.

Shortly after the parent conference, our class began oral book reports. Brian chose to read a book called *Rascal* by Sterling North. It was, I knew, a Newbery Honor winner, which meant its reading level was elementary school. But I let Brian read it because there was a childlike quality about him. He hadn't had a lot of the experiences of teenagers who lived a "normal" life. He was not worldly or socially mature. He hadn't dated, done much with pop culture, or learned to swear—at least, I hadn't heard him swear. He had been more isolated than other teenagers, so I decided he could read this book, and we'd see how he did.

"Brian," I began, "if you'd rather write a report, you may. I know it might be hard for you to give it orally. You know ... you might have some breathing problems."

"No," Brian said, "I'd like to do it orally."

"Really?"

"Yes. I just want to do it like everybody else."

"All right. But promise me that if it gets to be too much, you'll stop, and you can write the rest."

"I will," he said. Then he added mischievously, "Would you like to place a small wager on that?"

"No. I've seen you in action when you make up your mind. Besides, teachers don't make much money, and I have three little mouths to feed."

He smiled and wiggled in his chair.

"That's his sign that he's laughing inside," Kathy said. "He wiggles."

"All right, you win, Brian. But we'll make sure it's a good day when your breathing is working well. "

The class was quiet, listening to the whir of the electric wheelchair. Brian did a perfect circle and turned around to face us. I sat over at the side of the room, where I could see everything. Sometimes during oral book reports, I had to keep an eye on students who might cause a few distractions. But this time I didn't have to worry. Every eye was on Brian, and Brandy, Amy, B. J., and Pam were smiling encouragement. Brian was silent and looked across the room. Then he took a breath and began talking.

"The book *Rascal* was written by Sterling North. It's the story of a boy who takes care of a baby raccoon …" He paused after every few words and spoke so quietly that we strained to hear, but he continued on. "Sterling was lonely because his parents were often busy or gone." I looked around the room. My normally impatient students were hanging on his words. Brandy stared straight at Brian and sat back against the seat of her chair. B. J. was doodling on a sheet of paper, looking up every so often. Pam was smiling and trying to be encouraging. No one said a word. All we heard was Brian's halting voice. I noticed it was getting a bit slower, and his pauses for breath seemed to be coming more often. Should I stop him? I looked over at Kathy Gobbett and she was totally relaxed so I decided to stay calm. The clock had moved ten clicks when Brian started wrapping it up. "And so it is a timeless story about a boy and a pet, and I really liked it."

First there was silence; then everyone clapped, and Brian smiled and his eyes lit up. If he could have pointed at me, I know that he would have, making sure I knew he should have made that bet. He waited momentarily, as if he weren't quite sure what to do.

"Great job, Brian," I said. "Sounds like a book that really touched your funny bone."

"Yes," he responded. "I've been threatening my mom that I might get a raccoon."

"I'm sure that went over well."

"She said we'd have to add another bedroom, and she doesn't think that's possible right now."

I looked up to see if he was kidding and, as always, he smiled, and in his eyes was laughter. "Smarty. We have to go on to Ty next, so you'll have to give up center stage."

He moved the joystick, and the whirring machine came back to the side of the room, circled, and stopped. It had been an extraordinary event, listening to his report and watching him struggle, and I worked hard to keep my emotions in check as Ty walked up to the front.

Several weeks later that spring, Brian, Kathy, and I were in the room alone because the other kids were gone on a district testing day. Brian and Kathy were working on some homework, and I could hear her voice and Brian's quiet replies as I graded some papers. Pretty soon, Kathy asked if she could go to the office and make a call.

While she was gone, I asked Brian, "So, how are things going?"

"I think I've got a little too much homework to do tonight."

"Trying to make me feel guilty?"

He looked at me. "It's not working, is it?"

"Nope. But I am really kind of tired today myself. I didn't get much sleep last night because I kept having nightmares. Must have been something I ate."

Brian laughed. "Some nights are like that. Of course, people with a clean conscience don't have any difficulty sleeping. I sleep like a baby."

"You really are a troublemaker, aren't you?"

His eyes twinkled. Then he said, "Sometimes I do have dreams. And sometimes I can remember them, sometimes not."

"Me too. I often have dreams that happen in the house I grew up in. That house just stays in my subconscious. One of the houses we bought in Monmouth a few years ago was a house that I loved from the first time I walked through it. A few years later it hit me that it was laid out like the house where I grew up. Weird, huh?"

"Weird. I usually dream about the outdoors."

"Well, you did like that book you talked about and a lot of it was out in the woods."

"Sometimes I dream I'm out in the field at my grandparents' farm. Sometimes I'm fishing at their pond."

"That sounds really peaceful. Is your grandfather with you to help you?"

"No. Actually I'm running through the field, feeling the grass between my toes. And sometimes I dangle my feet in the pond and watch the frogs. I can hear the birds and smell the flowers. But mostly I can run."

I was silent.

"It's a pretty amazing feeling, and the wind hits my face and the bushes make rustling noises, and I run through the grass and find a shady tree. Then I lie down on my back and look at the clouds. They roll across the sky, and the sun shines down on my face. It's perfect."

We both sat silently for a moment.

"Does this dream happen very often?"

"Sometimes. It's a little different each time but some things are the same."

I reached over and put my hand on his, and before I could even stop my mouth, it asked, "So how do you feel about that?"

Brian looked at me. "Well, usually I wake up and realize I'm in my bed and, of course, it was just a dream. But you know, I think someday it'll happen. I really believe heaven doesn't have wheelchairs. I think I'll run." He paused for a few seconds. "Maybe the rooms are laid out like your house!"

I looked at him and saw that he was smiling. "Well, in that case, there will be an extra room for your raccoon."

During that semester I shared with Brian, I never lost my anxiety about his breathing. On days that weren't as good for him, he often appeared pale, and it was obvious he had a bit more trouble pulling in oxygen. He was unusually quiet on those days. Kathy took care of all of his needs, and I didn't really do much more than occasionally ask questions.

One day, however, we were discussing a poem called "First Lesson," when a student brought the message to my room that Kathy had a call in the office. She left to take the call, and I went back to the poem. "This entire poem is a metaphor, isn't it?" I asked. "For what?" It was quiet; no one raised his hand. My gaze swept the room, and I saw Brian's eyes, which silently said, *"I know the answer. Call on me."*

I didn't even stop to think. I walked over to his wheelchair, leaned over, and as if it were the most natural thing in the world, I put my hand over his tracheotomy.

He looked at me and said, "It's a metaphor for a child going out on his own. The father is hoping that he has taught her everything she needs to know for what's coming. And he knows he has to let her go so she can make her own way in the world, even though up to that point he has watched over her."

The room was silent. I took my hand away, stared into his eyes for a moment, and chuckled. Then I said, "Brian, that's the perfect answer." We looked at each other until I broke the moment, turned, and walked to the front of the room. When I sat down on my stool, I glanced back at Brian. His eyes were steady and clear. He blinked a couple of times as I looked straight into his face. I had somehow passed a test but I was the student and he, the teacher. The rest of the class was perfectly still.

I noticed the silence and said, "And that, ladies and gentlemen, is the last word on the poem 'First Lesson.'" About that time, Kathy slipped back in the door, and I gave the assignment for the next day. Brian turned his wheelchair and headed out the door a bit more slowly than usual. Then I looked up because his whirring chair changed course; he'd turned his wheelchair, and I thought he was going to ask me a question.

Instead, he looked intently at me, smiled broadly, and I understood what I had not when Brian Hendel first came into my life. This gentle, quiet soul had reminded me that human beings come in unique and varied packages, and my job—as another human being—was to help them do the best with the many talents they had. Then he was gone, and the other students began packing up their things.

In 2009 our local newspaper contained a letter to the editor that decried the time, effort, and money needed to mainstream students with developmental disabilities. The author felt that such students would be better off in institutions, and "normal" students would be better off with the classroom teacher's full attention. Even though his disability wasn't developmental, Brian came to my mind, and I thought about how happy he had been in my class.

Jim Keefe, who is a vice president of Warren Achievement Center—a facility designed to help people with developmental disabilities (DD) achieve their full potential as members of the community—posted a reply in an editorial. In part, it read:

> There is an additional cost to society when people with disabilities are segregated into institutions: the people living outside the institution miss the opportunity to know and appreciate the struggles and triumphs of the person with DD. Those in the mainstream become less likely to learn tolerance for others. In a society segregated by intelligence, the so-called "normal" child learns that it is proper to deny freedom and opportunity to people with lesser abilities. Freedom and opportunity are the deepest of American values. Remember also, Jesus taught, "whatever you did for one of the least of these brothers of mine, you did for me." (Matthew 40)

Not "Rest in peace, Brian," but instead, "Run, Brian, run!"

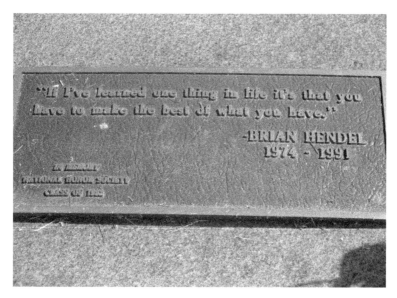

Brian's memorial at MHS. "If I've learned one thing in life, it's that you have to make the best of what you have."
Brian Hendel, 1974–1991

Part III

Elder Stateswoman
(1990s)

Chapter Thirteen

The Mirror of His High School Eyes

I looked down the long aisle of baby food, diapers, and comic books, and seeing no one, I drummed my fingers on the cash register. It was July and business wasn't exactly brisk at 2:00 PM on a Saturday. The summer of 1991, I learned that being a checker in a grocery store was *not* going to be my permanent summer vocation.

With my oldest child going to college in the fall, I figured I should supplement my modest teacher's salary with summer work to help pay his college bills. I usually worked in the summer anyway, but in the past, that job consisted of teaching at College for Kids. This summer, however, after twenty-three years at the local high school and another ten summers at College for Kids, I felt like it was time to scope out other vocational heights.

This wasn't an easy job in our little town of only 9,900 people. Couldn't paint houses because I was allergic to paint; couldn't mow lawns because I was allergic to pollen. Our small town library didn't need help, and roofing and building construction were not exactly in my line as a high school English teacher. However, this grocery story was only a half-block from my house, and I reasoned that I could work here part-time and still be home part-time to keep an eye on my semi-adult children.

My older son, the college-bound scholar, was also working this summer, as he had all through high school. He understood that he had to help pay for his college education. Unlike me, however, he worked at the leisurely paced, sunshine-filled local golf course. His evenings were free—life was good.

So here I was, stacking boxes, sacking groceries, learning prices, and figuring out the cash register. That last job was harder than it appeared because our town hadn't yet heard of grocery scanners, and the cashiers had to keep a lot of information in their heads. I'd already discovered that my recent high school students were much better at doing this than I was—a piece of information that delighted them to no end. And my body had learned that all the turning from the cash register to sack groceries wasn't exactly back-friendly, especially when that back was forty-four years old. But, I reasoned, it was a job and maybe the back pain would go away—hopefully by August.

Despite my back, I found an interesting part of grocery checking was seeing the local constabulary catch shoplifters. In our economically depressed town, there were always a few of these, and on many occasions, the small-town, future "Fugitives of the Week" were my former students. I also brought a real plus to the management: I had a memory that knew which beer-laden teenagers were not yet twenty-one—obviously one of the talents that tipped the scales in hiring a high school English teacher as a grocery checker.

So here I was. It was quiet … too quiet. It did, however, give me some moments to reflect on our little town. Working here meant I saw most people in town several times a week. This was the place where moms gossiped across their over-packed carts, junior high girls sacked groceries to support their trip to cheerleading camp, and senior citizens came to buy their heart medicine and groceries, especially on Tuesdays, when they jammed the parking lot because they got a 10 percent discount. In the evening, this same parking lot was the turnaround point for the

'90s version of teenage cruising. Romances began, romances ended—apparently more noisily than they began—parties were planned, and directions were given to the latest house where the parents were out of town.

And to think that I was at the focal point of all this turbulent activity!

However, on this particular day in July, it was slow going. Not too many people in the store, and I was thinking I might end up getting to go home early since they wouldn't need me.

And then the unimaginable happened. Down my lane came Jack Harvey, a former student I hadn't seen for maybe fifteen years. I recognized him immediately and him, me.

"Hey! Mrs. Van Kirk, right? Great to see you!" He laid his groceries on the counter, shook my hand, and added, "Are you still teaching? You know, you don't look any different that you did when I was in school."

Did I really look this old back then? What a charmer he still was, which became clear as we talked. "Hi, Jack. I'd know you anywhere. Still the guy you were so many years ago when you were in my class. And yes, I'm still teaching, but working here for the summer. You know, change of pace. Gosh, it's been … what? Fifteen years? Haven't seen you around recently, so you must be visiting."

"We get back occasionally 'cause my mom still lives here, but my wife and I are living not far away, actually. St. Louis. Back for a class reunion at the high school. You know, I hate to tell you, but it's actually been twenty years."

Twenty years. It didn't seem possible. I searched Jack's face and silently considered the slight lines around his mouth and the occasional silver hairs that curled just above his ears. Suddenly I saw my old life through the mirror of his high school eyes. It was my second year of teaching, and I was only five years older than my seniors—clearly a scary thought. Those were the days when I was so, so young. I wore my hair in a long, dark-brown, blond-streaked flip, used plenty of brown eye shadow and mascara, and didn't have to worry about the toll of 2:00 AM feedings and diaper changing. That was me—the young teacher in school who pushed the limits of skirt lengths, attuned with the times. After all, those were the days of the miniskirt. *Geez, it's a miracle that Jack recognized me in my forty-four-year-old depreciated stage.*

But for now I checked him over. He was about the same height as I remembered (six foot to my five foot four), still slender, and he sported a dark brown ponytail. Heartbreaker back then; heartbreaker still.

In high school Jack was really quiet, and I kept wondering what was going on behind those eyes. I had had some rare and occasional hints that his thoughts, if he'd cared to share them, traveled far and deep. The old adage "Still waters run deep," flitted through my mind briefly. Back then, he had that gaunt, starving-artist look, a surefire attraction to plenty of blonde and brunette lovelies in the late '60s. He gave me an update on what happened to him after high school and as he talked, I remembered the quiet adolescent who was part of a group of twenty-three boys and one girl—the class I taught at 8:00 AM, five days a week, 182 days, twenty fast years ago—the blink of an eye.

Good thing business was slow, because we probably talked for ten minutes. The conversation wound down, and he was about to leave. But just before grabbing his grocery sacks and heading out the door, Jack turned to me and—obviously emboldened by the warm and glowing thoughts of yesteryear—said a truly astonishing thing:

"You know what I remember the most about your class?" He smiled broadly and my mind started to search for a good come-back to that. In my head, a drum roll began. This was the moment most teachers dreamed about—the returning student whose life was changed by her words of wisdom; the reformed miscreant who turned his life around because she believed in him; the former dropout who went back to school and got his GED, BA, MA, and PhD because she told him to never, *never* give up on his dreams.

I smiled.

It didn't get much better than this.

After all those years of college, all those times of struggling to pay my bills, all those moments of wondering if it was all worth it to spend my life teaching, all those worries that I'm wasn't helping them enough—it all boiled down to this life-affirming instant for the typical teacher. Ah, one of those times when you hoped he was remembering how you changed his life.

So I said nonchalantly, "Gosh, after all these years? What stayed in your mind, Jack?"

And Jack Harvey looked me right in my forty-four-year-old eyes and said with a smile, "You've got great legs."

Chapter Fourteen

Mr. Vonnegut and Me

Part I

When Gary Collins, high school principal, wandered into my English classroom just before Thanksgiving, I should have suspected a difficult conversation would ensue. He studied my bulletin board on Twain and *Huckleberry Finn* while I finished talking with a student. Then he simply sat down in a desk near the door and patiently waited. After the student left, he looked at me, smiling, and said, "Sue Abbadusky. [That was my married name at the time]. Gotta minute?"

It's always a bad sign when the principal says that. I dropped into a desk next to him. "Sure."

I didn't anticipate that this "minute" would set in motion a drama that would witness my name and reputation dragged through five newspapers, one metropolitan television station, and our small town. Then there was, of course, that amazing, shocking, and generous gift at the end of it all. But this remarkable and unexpected turn of events began, simply, with "Gotta minute?"

Gary had a deceptive calm in the middle of controversy. He was about my age, forty-nine, and his physical presence was impressive. When he stood, his six-foot-two-inch frame was a solid obstacle. Occasionally, he used wily humor to dispel disagreements. Skillful in handling controversy, he typically began to probe for information with a neutral question: "Are your students reading books for a book report right now?"

"*Always*, Gary. Why?"

"Well, I'm curious about your book report policy. Humor me. Do students pick their own books, or do you recommend them, or do they have certain books they're required to read?"

I glanced at his inscrutable face. I smiled. "Depends. Which class?"

He momentarily looked at the photo of Mark Twain tacked to my bulletin board, studied it carefully, and then looked back at me. "American lit? Oh, right—Twain."

"We're reading *Huckleberry Finn*. We're writing book reports on outside reading." I pondered his possible motive with this interview. "I know why you're asking all these questions. You want to come in and talk about growing up on the river in Dallas City—Mark Twain's river. Gotcha. Anything to get back in the classroom."

Gary chuckled. "Gee, good guess but not exactly." We sat in silence for a few seconds. "So? Do you have a required reading list?" He looked directly into my eyes, determined to guide the conversation back to some as-yet-undeclared focus.

"A reading list, yes. It has college-bound books on it. But they can choose something else, as long as I okay it. Why all these questions? Looking for a good book to read over Thanksgiving?"

"Ah, well, you almost guessed it." His smile disappeared, and his face and good natured manner switched to a more serious note. "I had a parent in my office today who was upset about a book her daughter is reading for your class."

Now we came to the heart of the matter. "Oh, really? Which book?"

"Something called *Breakfast of Champions*. Vonnegut, maybe? Sound right?"

"Well, I have seventy students reading books now, but she could be reading that. It's one of the books on the list. Who's the student? What's the problem?"

"Jim Kroner's wife was in, and she claims that her daughter came to you and said she didn't want to read this Vonnegut book because it contained all kinds of obscene stuff. Actually, I believe her word choice was 'gross.' It's her contention that you're making her child read this book. I don't think it sounds like something you'd do, and I said so." He looked up, smiling. "*Are* you making her child read this book?"

I looked over Gary's shoulder and stopped to think about his question. "Now that you mention it, she did appear before class one day and said she didn't understand her book. But she'd already written a really perceptive book report on *The Catcher in the Rye*, so I figured she could handle this book. Besides, the due date for the report was coming up fast. I told her I'd research and retrieve some secondary essays on the book and that would help her figure out his points. But it's not required. It's a book report book. Doesn't her mother know it was a choice?"

"I'm not sure. Mrs. Kroner looked at the book and says it has … ah … all kinds of sexual cartoons, objectionable language, and a lot of things that are suggestive and inappropriate for a teenager. She called it 'pornographic.'"

I could feel my anxiety level rising and my blood pressure following. "You have to be kidding. Vonnegut's books, even this one, are on most college-bound lists." I stopped dead, digesting this morsel of information and then raised a question. "Did you tell her that I don't require them to read a specific book? She could easily read something else."

"I had a feeling that's what you'd say. I told her I believed that was your policy, but I'd investigate. And I assured her that I knew how you operated, and if the book offended her daughter, you'd be willing to have her read a different book and get full credit…So now I'm investigating, as I promised. I have to tell you, she was more than upset.

I explained that we've had these situations come up before, particularly in social studies and science. Usually, we've made sure the student could find something more acceptable. I also pointed out that Vonnegut was an important author, widely read. Students in American lit need to be exposed to varied writing."

"'Varied writing,' huh? We'd better find her daughter a different book. Plenty of other books on the list have absolutely nothing that anyone could find objectionable. I'll get on it. You want me to call the parents?"

"No, I'll do that tomorrow morning," Gary said, rising from his chair. "Have her switch the book. Meanwhile, look over the list and figure out something else that would work for her."

"Sure. No problem."

Gary moved toward the door and turned, as if to underscore his thoughts. "Oh, and Mrs. Kroner also indicated that she would be going to the superintendent's office. So it's possible—I mean, it sure could be that we haven't heard the end of it."

That was November 21. I didn't think that it would go much beyond talking with the girl the next day and offering her some other alternatives. And that was exactly what I did, with little ceremony or discussion. I gave her four or five books that were calculated to offend no one, and she looked them over and chose one. Careful not to say anything that might distress her or make her parents more upset than they already were, I also extended the report deadline because she'd need more time to read. With that, I figured the matter was finished and didn't give it another thought.

The following day, Collins visited me once again, this time bearing a daunting stack of paper and a paperback book. Mrs. Kroner had returned the school board policy form that was required when a parent objected to educational materials. Along with the form, she had given back the school library's copy of *Breakfast of Champions*, dog-eared, falling apart at the binding, much read, and occasionally loved—but not this time.

She had completed the form with large black letters, leaving no doubt of her viewpoint. In her mind, the book was "pornographic and contained obscenities, racial slurs, and filth." It would warp our children. *Our* children? Her opinion was that the book had no educational value for any age group. In answering the form's questions, she explained that she was not aware of the judgment of the book by educational authorities, but she believed that its theme was "pornography and trash." Attached to the form was a packet of thirty-eight pages, photocopied from various parts of the Vonnegut novel. A black marker had been liberally used to circle or underline sentences or line-drawn Vonnegut cartoons that were evidently pornographic. Her recommendation was that the book be withdrawn from all students.

No wishy-washy opinions here.

Gary asked me about the book. Years earlier, he had read it but only vaguely remembered it. So I explained that yes, it did have obscene words, racial slurs, and sexual references. I doubted that Gary or I had been warped by reading it. Vonnegut's book was published shortly after we were in college, and we'd read it then, rather than when we were sixteen years old. I had also read *Slaughterhouse-Five*—another often-censored Vonnegut book—when it appeared in 1969.

Many of my former students had read and loved *Breakfast*. But as I considered those students, I realized they had been strong readers and intellectual thinkers. All had been mature for their age and, most importantly, they had had a wicked sense of humor. I checked the past book reports of the offended student, and it appeared that she had consistently chosen, read, and understood college-bound books. Both *The Catcher in the Rye* and *To Kill a Mockingbird* were on her reading card during the previous year. I saw no indication from her past reading that books that contained strong language or racial prejudice offended her. However, Vonnegut's book was filled with sexual references and perhaps those were the sticking point. So I had to concede that if that were the real problem, a different book would be the answer. On the other hand, removing the Vonnegut book from the clutches of my other students was not an option I could tolerate. I had students who could not only read *Breakfast* but who understood clearly Vonnegut's viewpoint.

I had never failed to go along with the wishes of any parent with objections to what his child was reading. But over the twenty-eight years I'd taught, few parents had objected. Only two had returned books and contacted me. One asked that her son not read *Flowers for Algernon* by Daniel Keyes, because of a brief sexually explicit scene. I said, "No problem," and we located a different book. On another occasion, a parent had come to school and returned a copy of *Catch-22* by Joseph Heller. She felt her son didn't need to be influenced by the violence of war. No problem. In both cases, I would have been extremely upset if the parents had said, "Don't let anyone else's kid have access to this book." But no one had said that. Until now.

Over Thanksgiving break I had two children home from college, plus my high school son. In my mind the discussion was over, and Vonnegut's book was now in the hands of Marilyn Black, school librarian. The binding needed some work, and Marilyn set about using some glue to salvage it.

On Monday my older children returned to college, and I shifted my attention to school. I didn't realize that this week would mark the beginning of what I'd label "Face Time with Multiple Administrators Week." First, I received a polite summons to the principal's office.

I sat down in Gary's office, and he handed me some papers. "Mrs. Kroner went to the superintendent's office after she spoke with me. This is a letter she brought in, and they also sent a copy to the school board. I'll give you a few minutes to read it."

As I perused the first page of the letter to the superintendent, Don Jenkins, I saw that the parents had outlined the basics of the "situation." The letter revealed that the girl asked me if I'd read the book and I answered, "Yes, but it's been a few years." I clearly remembered that. I skimmed a few more lines and started thinking out loud. "Okay, wait a minute. She says her daughter said what? I don't remember her saying anything about the book's being 'gross.' I remember asking her if she *understood* it. Otherwise, why offer to give her some information on the themes of the book? I'm not sure, Gary, where this conversation came from. Let me think a minute ... No, my own memory was that she said she didn't understand the book. She had already tried another book and didn't like it, so she changed to the Vonnegut book."

"So, let me get this straight," Gary said. "It was your understanding that she had a problem with figuring out what the book was saying? You don't recall her telling you the book was 'gross' or 'disgusting'?"

"No, not at all. However, I do notice that her parents believe that's what she said, and the first page of this letter mentions that *the parents* feel it is not only pornographic but also disgusting. This puzzles me; I wouldn't have left her with a book she described as 'gross.'"

And now my eyes scanned down to the later paragraphs of the letter. "They are questioning not only the board's policy for putting materials in the learning centers but also asking who makes the decisions regarding these books. I assume our librarian has a policy for book selection?"

"Absolutely. We have a clear policy stating what Marilyn can put into the district libraries. If it comes to that, I'll get you a copy." He looked at a handwritten list on his desk and inquired, "Maybe you'd better explain how you came up with this list of books for your classes. Obviously, I should know that." He smiled. "Slowly—I'm taking notes."

"Well, I have a list of American writers for my American literature classes. My honors class also has a list. When Jan Willhardt and I set up these class lists, we consulted not only two professors in the English department at Monmouth College, but also used the books recommended by a poll of the English departments of state colleges and universities—and the National Council of Teachers of English. We used their list too. So it's a combination of those three sources. And—you'll love this—my American lit classes are currently reading *Huckleberry Finn*, and one of the topics we'll examine is the censorship history of that book. We'll even watch a film concerning book censorship and school board policies.

"Gary, it makes a lot of sense to me to call the Kroners and ask them to come in and talk with me. I'm sure I can explain the situation, and I don't know many subjects that are too scary to discuss. I know she's been in your office, but neither parent has talked with me. What do you think?"

"Sounds fine. I'll give them a call and see if they can come in after school later in the week. I'll sit in on the conversation as an extra pair of ears."

During the next couple of days as I taught my classes, I was particularly mindful that not only was my son in one of my American lit classes with many of his friends, but also that the Kroner's daughter was in the same class. I didn't approach her to discuss anything other than her progress on the new book. We continued to discuss *Huck Finn*, but I knew, as my son put it, that students were aware that something was "going on" with the Kroner girl's book report. Normally, gossip travels at lightning speed in a small town.

Later that day, Gary Collins mentioned to me that the Kroners would come in Thursday after school.

"Okay," I thought. "We'll get this straightened out."

On Wednesday after school, I came back to my classroom from the office to find yet another administrator sitting in a student desk. This time it was the superintendent, Don Jenkins. One of the complicating ironies of this whole book controversy was the innate spider web of connections with overlapping relationships. I had taught two of the Jenkins' daughters, both of Gary Collins' daughters, both of Jim Kroner's sons, and the friends of both my son and the Kroner's daughter. This small-town dimension made neutrality difficult. Even the members of the school board had children who were or had been in my classes. I'd only missed having the board president as a student by a couple of years.

"Hello, Dr. Jenkins. Just a matter of time, wasn't it, before I spoke with you? Don't suppose you're selling Girl Scout cookies for your wife again. I guess you're here about the book. ... I think it's under control."

"Never a doubt in my mind, Sue. However, I thought I'd mosey over here from my office and have a few words with you. Just checking in, so to speak. How are you doing?"

What a kindness that he would wonder how I was feeling.

Don Jenkins had been superintendent for three years and except for teaching his daughters, I'd not had much contact with him. He was probably in his fifties, soft spoken, and methodical. He always thought carefully before he spoke, and his words were spoken slowly and cautiously. He also researched from top to bottom before he made decisions. To me, he'd always been cordial.

"I've certainly had better days. I think this has been a huge misunderstanding and when the parents come in tomorrow to talk with Gary and me, I'm sure we'll get this cleared up."

"Good. How is their daughter doing?"

"Seems to be fine. I keep my distance, although I call on her occasionally in class."

He looked down at some papers he had on the desk and seemed to be thinking about how he would say his next words. "I have a feeling this may be about more than the Vonnegut book. I spoke with the parents. Sounds like they're concerned with the books in the library."

"What?" I was incredulous.

"They're concerned the district may have more books like the Vonnegut book that they would not want students to read." He looked up at me over the top of his reading glasses, which were perched on the end of his nose.

I protested, "Surely the Kroners realize that only their own child's reading is up to them. Do they really think they should decide what other people's kids can read?"

"From their statements, I believe they might be considering simply removing books."

Shaking my head in disbelief, I straightened my shoulders and said with as much conviction as I could muster, "This conference tomorrow will clear up everything."

"Well, I hope so." Now I was worried because it sounded like he had some understanding that I didn't have. He paused, looked beyond me, and then cleared his throat. "However, in the meantime I'd like you to do something for me."

"Sure, anything."

"I'd like you to sit down and write a description. Tell me the circumstances surrounding the book report assignment. Give me what your expectations were. Tell me what transpired as far as your recollection of your conversation with the student. Finally, explain how you composed the reading list and why this book, in particular, was on the list." He cleared his throat. "Oh, and then if you could discuss the book's themes and why it's a good book for college-bound students, that would be helpful. I thought if it came to a meeting with the board, I'd have some information to give them."

He looked down, using his fingers to crease the corners of his papers on the desk. After some thought, he raised his eyes and said more forcefully, "Now don't get me wrong. I have every confidence in your ability to make these decisions, and I know, from experience, that your judgment is sound. I'm 100 percent behind you. I'm hoping, of course, that this conference tomorrow will solve the situation, and the parents will be satisfied. But if that doesn't happen, it would be wise for you to write this while details are still fresh in your mind." He took a deep breath, almost a sigh. "Sometimes things get mixed up following this sort of complaint. These parents have called at least one school board member that I know of and maybe more. Think you could take care of that and send both Gary and me a copy? If this whole thing gets more tangled, it would be good to have a clear picture before time confuses things."

I was feeling rattled by the direction of this conversation. I hadn't thought about the situation intensifying. I said, "Sure. And I appreciate your advice. You'll have the paper tomorrow morning, and I'll copy one to Gary. Thank you, Dr. Jenkins, for your support."

He rose. "No, thank *you*. Now I don't want you to worry. We'll assume tomorrow will assure the parents that we're aware of their concerns."

After he left my room, I sat there in thought for quite some time.

On Thursday afternoon, Jim Kroner came through the door of my classroom followed by Gary Collins. Slow and methodical, Jim usually spoke softly and cautiously. A tall, angular man with impressive silver hair, he put me in mind of an undertaker or a minister. His demeanor and body language inspired confidence and, because he was a businessman, I suppose that was a good thing.

I said hello and smiled, but he didn't smile back. *Well, so much for the pleasantries*, I thought. I moved to arrange some chairs in a circle and wondered why his wife wasn't with him. We sat down, Jim facing me a few feet away and Gary to the left of me and between us.

Gary folded his hands on his desk. "Thanks for coming in, Jim," he began slowly and easily. "I hope we can resolve some of these issues. I know Sue suggested we call and see if maybe some conversation would take care of this. And we have a school policy not only for acquiring materials but also for committee review when parents have concerns. We're going to send this book to that committee, and they'll get back to us shortly with whether or not this book meets the district policy. But we're both glad you accepted our invitation to come in and talk. It's always good to exchange viewpoints."

Jim looked at us and began to speak quietly. "I've known both of you for quite a long time, Gary." He looked at me and continued, "And you've taught my two boys. I will always feel very good about how the teachers here at the school—and the coaches—worked with my kids, especially my older son. I know, Sue, you put a lot of time in with him, trying to help him."

I waited for the "but," and he didn't disappoint.

He looked back down at the desk top and spread the fingers of each hand on the flat surface. "But I have to tell you this is a totally different situation with this book." His words were slow and clear. "This book" came out with obvious distaste. He spoke in a tightly contained way, holding in his feelings. His voice never wavered or rose. "I don't know how you can defend having such a coarse, ugly piece of pornography in a library used by our children. These are just kids—thirteen, fourteen, maybe a little older. I looked at this book." He glanced up at Gary. "Did you look at the pages my wife copied, Gary?"

"Yes, I did, Jim."

"How can you begin to explain how such a piece of filth could be in a school library? For that matter, it makes us wonder if there are other books of the same tenor in the schools."

"Well, Jim—" Gary began.

Jim raised his hand, indicating he wasn't finished. "I want you to know we see ourselves as good parents." He shifted his weight and turned toward Gary. "We keep an eye on our daughter. When she leaves the house, we know who she's with and where she's going. If she's going to be late getting home or something comes up, she calls us. We *always* know where she is. And that's the same reason we check what she's reading for school and the movies she goes to see with her friends. We aren't for all the violence and sex and four-letter, vulgar words you see or hear in movies." He paused a moment, although he still hadn't raised his voice. "But to think that right here in our school—the one we pay taxes for, right here—we find a book like this." With each pause between clauses, he used a pointed finger on the desk to punctuate his words. "How can you condone such a book? How can you have students read this in your class? Our daughter told us she was disgusted, offended, and upset that she had to read this book and—"

Now it was my turn to interrupt. "She didn't have to read this book, Jim, nor was it ever assigned to her. It's on a book list for college-bound students. The choice is optional. It's recommended by colleges and universities as one of *many* books students should read before they go to college. Vonnegut is considered an important American author."

His voice amplified, becoming more emotional. "I can't understand that. How can such filthy words and pictures—oh, my gosh—have you looked at the pictures in that book? How can you let children read such things?" And now it was obvious that it was time to consider the book.

"Are you familiar with the author, Vonnegut, or his writing?"

"Why would I want to be? This is just awful stuff. I don't understand. Why have a book like this on school book lists and in children's libraries?"

"Jim, it isn't in children's libraries. This is a *high school* library. These teenagers will soon be in college. The reason *Breakfast of Champions* is on the reading list is that it's recommended by experts as a strong piece of writing that students should read before they go to college. Another novel of Vonnegut's, *Slaughterhouse-Five*, has also caused a great deal of controversy."

"I suppose that's in the library, too?"

"Yes, and also highly recommended for high school reading. How can you teach people to think if they only read what they agree with?" I finished.

Agree. I think it must have occurred to him that I wasn't agreeing with his viewpoint. Now his voice began to modulate more. "Tell me what's worthwhile in this so-called 'important' book? Why would you defend such a piece of trash? After my wife saw what awful filth is in that book, she showed it to me, and I was appalled. What is the socially redeeming message of such a book?"

Taking a deep breath, I measured my words. "Kurt Vonnegut loves to be offensive." Mr. Kroner started to speak, but I quickly went on. "This book is satire that Vonnegut uses to skewer all the things he hates about modern American culture. By making readers angry, he gets them to think. I understand that you're conservative and concerned about the best course of action for your daughter. But even though this *Breakfast of Champions* is pretty bleak and dark, I think you'd agree with some of his themes." I was beginning to feel the tension that sometimes cropped up between my shoulder blades when I was stressed.

"You have to be kidding."

"Not really." I shook my head. "Vonnegut's being critical of our values, our popular culture, advertising, and other things he calls 'junk.' Look at the preface—you can get a pretty good idea of his complaints:

killing people in useless wars, language that debases people, slavery, greed as a national value, the destruction of nature through our pollution."

"That wasn't what I saw in that book. I saw—"

"I know. You saw 'dirty words and filthy pictures.' He wants you to understand that something beautiful like sex has been turned into dirty jokes. He's against degrading other people because of their race or using four-letter words crudely when language can be such an amazing, subtle tool. We have choices about how we'll live and so far, we've done an awful job. He believes we need to rethink our values. The lit class your daughter is in tries to prepare kids for college reading by helping them understand that as the times change, so does the style of writing. This book is from the postmodern period and so, yes, it has violence, four-letter words, and sharp, often offensive ideas. That's part of that period of time in literature." I was watching his face as I spoke, and something hard and definite was resolving itself. Maybe he understood what I said, but he was having none of it.

"I don't think my daughter needs to explore that period of time, nor do other children who are thirteen, fourteen, fifteen. That book is filled with pornographic cartoons and terrible language. There's no value in that. And for that matter I am shocked and disappointed that you'd think this is a good book for your students." He caught his breath and then said quietly, "I have to say, I thought I knew what you stood for, but I am deeply disappointed in your moral values, Sue."

Gary could see on my face that I was stunned by this announcement.

Gary looked back and forth at both of us. "Well, I think we're probably done here …" But before I could say anything else, Jim Kroner beat me to it. And now his quiet voice did rise considerably.

"Yes, we're done for now. I'll be very clear. My wife and I want this book out of the school library. We pay taxes for this school, and we should have a say in what our children are exposed to. We'll go to the school board and, if they don't agree, I promise you—*I promise you*—we will use the media to show what's going on in our school libraries. I personally know the governor, and I will not hesitate to contact him and put enough pressure on this school district that this will not happen again. I'll contact the State Board of Education. You'll see. I have friends who are influential. And we'll also contact the NAACP. When they hear the racist remarks in this book, you'll see what happens when you defend such a piece of trash. I'll go to the newspapers, the television stations, and we'll get something done. We will go into the learning centers in the district and clean out all the filth and trash. We'll get the parents organized to do this. We pay taxes, and we won't stop until we have this trash cleared out of our schools."

That was the wrong thing to say. Now Gary, who had been quiet during this "worthwhile exchange of meaningful viewpoints," spoke calmly, all the while under tense control.

"That's not going to happen, Jim. Certainly you and all parents have a right to question decisions, but you don't make decisions about what will be included in school libraries. And we won't be bullied by threats to bring in the media or censorship police of any sort. We'll let the committee do its work, and you'll have to do whatever you believe you need to do. But for now, we're done talking."

Clear, definite, decisive. Gary quickly stood up. Jim stood up. Before I knew it, they were out the door and headed back down toward the office. I sat quietly for a few minutes, although shaking with anger. I felt cold all over, and I crossed my arms and leaned forward a bit. I could not believe he had said those things. And the statement that really made me angry was his questioning of *my* values. It wasn't really personal until that statement. Unbelievable. I took some deep breaths and considered what might happen next. The National Guard burning books on the lawn? And then my mood lightened. How amazing. Kurt Vonnegut, you've sure put me in the stew here. I was still shaking my head when Gary came back into my room.

"You okay?"

"Sure. But I can't believe, first of all, that he'd be so threatening over a book, and second, that he wants to censor all kinds of books in the library. That's crazy. If he took out every book that might have four-letter words or violence or sex, most of the books written in the last half century would be gone. And for that matter, so would the *Bible*. Do you think he really means what he says? Going into the learning centers? Removing books?"

"Possibly. Could be he'll calm down and realize we're trying to be reasonable about his daughter's assignment. Guess we'll have to wait and see where this is going."

Two days later, Saturday morning, I padded out to my front porch in my bathrobe and slippers, coffee in hand, and picked up my copy of the local newspaper, the *Daily Review Atlas*. As I unrolled it and headed back into my house, I was dismayed by the headline: "Controversy Arises Over Book at Monmouth High School." I didn't remember talking to the local newspaper. I opened up the front page and began reading. An editor's note in italics explained: *"The following story, concerning the objections raised about a book used for course credit by a Monmouth High School teacher, does not contain the title of the book concerned, the names of the student, and/or teacher involved. The* Review Atlas *purposefully withheld this information in order to avoid holding any individual up to ridicule and scorn; and in an effort to avoid drawing undo attention to the literature being discussed."* It was followed with a byline from "Executive Editor" John R. Stiles. *Hmmm*, I thought. *Interesting journalistic practice.* "Ridicule and scorn?" That's pretty humorous. Evidently that means guilty as charged. And with a school of 500 students, I'll bet no one can guess whose English class is involved. Or which book. Or which student.

The article went on to describe the "controversy." It explained that a letter had been "hand-delivered" to members of the school board and that a set of parents had "lodged a formal complaint" about "a mid-1970s novel by an American author." A number of photocopied pages had been sent by the parents to the Regional Office of Education, the high school principal, the school board, and other principals in the district. Incorrectly, the article stated the parents had met with a board of educators "who rule on the appropriateness of books contained within the school's library," and that the superintendent had been "drawn into the fray." Fray? What fray? What board of educators? So far the school had made no official comment, according to the article, and the newspaper thought perhaps a committee of educators was studying this controversy—ah, an accurate statement. But it was clear that the parents wanted the book out of the library and would do "whatever it takes" to cause that event. They also planned to get a team of people, either educators or parents, to "'clean out any other pornographic trash' supplied to our children." Using the word "supplied" made it sound like something quite illegal, like supplying lines of cocaine. Unbelievable.

Since we had had our meeting with Jim Kroner on Thursday, this information must have already been delivered to the newspaper. Why immediately send it to the newspapers when the district had a policy and framework for reviewing the materials? And where was that old journalistic practice of getting both sides of the story? Had anyone called me? No. Gary Collins? No. Obviously the agenda was to put pressure on the school board to ban the book and to let people go in and throw materials out of the libraries. Oh, and the newspaper would probably sell a few copies with this story, too.

Viewpoint was, unfortunately, being created.

Later that day I opened a folder with a copy of the school policy on library materials. It had been adopted a few years earlier by a school board that included Hallie Lemon—a former high school English teacher, a current college English professor, and an activist for protecting the right to read. Numbered as policy #6510-1, it was clear in its provisions. It began with a philosophy that decried narrowness in selecting library materials and promoted a "wide variety of education materials" and "the freedom to read." The principal and librarian were responsible for selecting books for the library. In order to promote "sound literary quality" the books must be recommended by a number of sources such as *Book Review Digest* or the *Literary Journal*. Several other sources were listed. So when the committee met, they would need to make sure the Vonnegut book was developmentally appropriate for high school according to these "unimpeachable sources."

It described topics that are often subject to criticism: religion, ideologies, sex, and science. Books that included sex should be "subjected to a stern test of literary merit and reality by the librarian." In other words, sexual incidents or profanity shouldn't mean automatically throwing such books out of the library. The librarian would have to make a decision based on the literary value of the book. If one of these "unimpeachable critical sources" considered a book acceptable, then that book selection was "not open to criticism or re-evaluation." That seemed to be a clear course of action for the committee and librarian.

On the following Monday, December 4, Gary asked me to be on the three-person review committee with Marilyn Black, the librarian, and Mary White, a chemistry teacher. I objected, saying it might make more sense to have someone else on the committee from my department—there were five of us—but he said as department chairman it should be me. I decided I wouldn't talk but instead would let my two colleagues do the talking.

That evening the *Daily Review Atlas* once again had stories about the "book controversy" and had contacted the superintendent's office. They had been told that a committee was reviewing the placement of *Breakfast of Champions* in the school library.

Now, however, new and breaking information was made public by the *Daily Review Atlas*. Their story explained that the parents had contacted the newspaper saying that "other concerned parents" had become involved in the controversy and would be meeting later in the week to discuss the situation. The book was back at the school "and the teacher who made the assignment defended the use of the work, which contained very graphic sexual and racial references." Interesting. Along with the December 4 story on the front page of the newspaper, Mr. Stiles also ran an editorial titled "Book Controversy Swirls." His editorial called for a quick, adult handling of the situation. I could agree with that call!

Mr. Stiles' editorial explained: "The book is anything but age appropriate for high school. And we believe it would be the rare student at that level who would be mature enough to handle the subject matter of this piece of literature." I knew several high school students who had read the book and understood it clearly, and his editorial had just insulted them. The editor went on to explain:

> The book in question is extremely graphic and raw as far as content, and we would venture a guess that there wouldn't be one in a hundred high school students who'd be able to understand anything beyond the earthy language it contains, let alone the meaning of the work. In fact, we doubt that there are one in a hundred high school teachers, principals and/or school administrators who could do the same."

Mr. Stiles ended the editorial with references to "a witch hunt or book-burning rally" and mentioned again that they wouldn't pinpoint the title of the book in order "to avoid the possibility of turning this into a promotional scheme for the book itself." Of course, by now the title of the book, as well as the author's name, spread like an epidemic throughout the area. The public library didn't have a copy, and Mrs. Black was gluing pages back into the spine of the school library copy. The closest book store in Galesburg didn't have a copy. Adolescents had heard of this wicked novel, but couldn't get their hands on a copy of it. If there had been copies available, they would have been flying off the shelves.

Stiles' editorial questioned the appropriateness of the book for high school students. This was probably a good topic to consider, because the officers of the National Council of Teachers of English were discussing it in Champaign, Illinois. After the NCTE sent its findings to the high school, it was obvious that the newspaper editor and the English teacher's professional organization were at odds.

That very day the Deputy Executive Director of NCTE, Mr. Charles Suhor, dictated a letter to Gary Collins. Gary had contacted him for a professional assessment of the suitability of *Breakfast of Champions* for high school students. Consequently, Suhor sent a letter to Gary and carbon-copied it to me. When this arrived, I felt like we had some official and professional help with this censorship issue. Mr. Suhor said that he would be pleased to comment on the novel from the "viewpoint of the National Council of Teachers of English."

In speaking for that organization, Mr. Suhor began with a description of how many people were standing with him: 130,000 members; 130 regional, state, and local affiliates with membership totals of 50,000, including the Illinois Association of Teachers of English with over 1,500 members. In short, most people interested in improving the quality of instruction in the English language were members of these organizations. So what did they think of the suitability of *Breakfast of Champions* for high school readers?

> As I understand it, the parent protesting the use of *Breakfast of Champions* objected to offensive language and sexual depictions in the book. It is clear, however, that the language and situations in this novel, as in any text under study, must be seen in the context of the entire work. The ethical and literary value of a work is distorted if one focuses only on particular words, passages, or sections. An author's broad vision, total treatment of theme, and commitment to realistic portrayal of characters and dialogue are ignored when protestors focus only on segments that are offensive to them.
>
> Further, it would be erroneous to assume that literary depictions of negative events, profane language, and the like are being endorsed by the author, the teacher, or the school. In fact, classroom study provides a fertile ground for students to interpret surface aspects of a literary work and to exercise thinking as they discuss characters and issues in the work. *Breakfast of Champions* lends itself well to such study in senior high schools.

It is a widely heralded work, cited in NCTE's 1976 high school *Books for You* list as a "self-satirizing novel," and it has been well reviewed in the literary criticism community.

I understand that two admirable policies related to the current situation are in place in your district. One is that a student can be given a choice of reading a substitute work if that student or his/her parents find a particular work objectionable. I further understand that the Vonnegut novel was one of the many choices available to students, and they were informed that they could change their selections if they found a work offensive. This is as fair and open a practice as I have seen in my contacts with hundreds of schools.

NCTE supports the right of parents to guide their own children's reading; but we believe that it is patently undemocratic for a parent or group of parents to foreclose on the right of *other* parents to guide *their* own children's readings, as is apparently being suggested by the protestor in your situation.

Your district's policy for a review of challenges to instructional materials is the kind of procedure that attends to substantive concerns of parents in a fair and orderly manner. We urge the review committee to retain *Breakfast of Champions* as a curriculum offering, and we urge that your Board of Education continue to work within sound policies of review.

Gary put a copy of Mr. Suhor's letter in my teachers lounge mailbox, and he also sent a copy to the superintendent and the school board members. However, the following day there was a letter to the editor of the local newspaper signed "Parents Who Care!" It described the pornographic nature of the book in question and quoted from the school district's board policy that pertained to adopting materials for the school libraries. It explained that the book in question had no literary quality whatsoever, and it asked all concerned "parents, grandparents and citizens of our community who care about our young people" to meet at the YMCA on December 7, 1995, from 7:00 to 9:00 PM. Once again the letter reiterated that the children of the community need support: "We as a community are supporting 'Just Say No to Drugs.' Let's also as a community 'Just Say No To Pornography in Our Schools!'"

None of us realized it at the time, but several of the high school students who had read Vonnegut's novel were not only angry with the newspaper editor for insulting their intelligence but also were planning to go to the announced meeting later in the week.

By this point it had been five days since the parent conference. During that time ...

- the town had seen two newspaper articles—and in neither case was I contacted for comment—and an editorial.
- the school had received a letter from the NCTE.
- I'd reviewed the school board's policies regarding selection of school materials.
- a faculty committee had been organized to review the policy and book in question.
- a committee of "concerned parents" was planning to meet.

I didn't realize then that this was only the tip of the iceberg. What began as a situation that I figured could be easily resolved was turning into a community nightmare, and the media was now steering the conversation. I felt the whole episode was out of control, and whatever happened next would occur because the Kroner family was contacting all forms of media and attempting to push their agenda through to take books out of the school libraries. It was a scary feeling—the thought that people in our community were reading information that affected their opinions of me and of the school district. What was truly strange during this period of time was that no one—and I repeat, *no one*—from the local newspaper contacted me regarding this story. The offended family was feeding their viewpoint to the media.

Carol Clark, a reporter for the *Galesburg Register-Mail*, did call and wanted to hear what I had to say concerning the story. Carol's subsequent news story made it clear that the book had a name, I had a name, and that Don Jenkins had received a letter from Jim and Cindy Kroner, who wanted to remove books from the libraries. The *Register-Mail*'s story began by quoting the Kroners, then described my viewpoint, and ended by quoting both the principal and superintendent. It was well-balanced.

That same day, December 6, the Monmouth newspaper contacted the principal and the superintendent. It ran a story titled "Initial decision on book is due later in the week." The newspaper said that the student told me the book was offensive, "at which time the teacher is supposed to have asked if the student understood the material and offered a synopsis of the book as help." As I read this information I kept saying to myself, "*Supposed* to have asked?" Why had no one called me and asked me if I truly did ask or offer that? And as of this newspaper report, no one realized I never heard the word "gross." Finally, the story mentioned that no formal announcement would be made when the decision came down from the school. Only the family would be notified.

The *Review Atlas* editorial on December 7 stated that the editor of the paper was in no way advocating the banning or burning of books. Then it went on to paint the student as a victim of a system that had cruelly misunderstood and abused her innocence. The argument rested on the initial conversation of the book's being gross, and it once again explained that I had used improper judgment in not directing the student immediately to another book. The final opinion of the whole column-long editorial was this: "If a student expresses the slightest offense or objection to optional material, run, don't walk to an alternate course of study." And, of course, the article ended with an appeal to the idea that we were all fighting on the same side: for our children and the future of our society.

Tear my hair out? Scream a few times? I was so angry at this one-sided picture of this whole situation that I just kept shaking my head in disbelief.

I was starting to think that maybe I should call the newspaper editor and explain my side of this whole discussion. But then I read a letter to the editor from one of my colleagues, and that convinced me that doing so would lead nowhere.

John Van Ausdall was an English teacher and colleague who taught expository writing, drama, speech, and debate classes at Monmouth High School. During this time, he was an officer of the school district's teachers union and in charge of representing any teacher who filed a grievance over working conditions. In other words, he was used to conflict management and persuasive differences. After reading the local newspaper coverage of the book issue and speaking with me, he decided to write a letter to the editor. It turned out to be the first of many letters of support written by colleagues, students, and community members. His letter read:

Dear Sir:

While I wholeheartedly agree with your assertion in the Monday, December 4, issue that, "Parents have the right to know just what their children are being exposed to at school," I am offended by the scurrilous implication that educators in Monmouth are somehow concealing an immoral curriculum. We, too, are parents and concerned citizens and have every bit as much at stake in our children's education as the next person. It is that not-so-subtle, anti-teacher tone and a couple of gross misrepresentations in Saturday's and Monday's papers that compel me to respond to Tuesday's editorial.

In the first place a misunderstanding needs to be corrected: The book in question is *not* required—of anyone—period. The book is, however, on a list of books compiled by the National Council of Teachers of English (a prestigious professional organization with approximately 65,000 members) recommended for college-bound 11th and 12th graders. Students in this class for the college bound are encouraged to select books from this list because colleges and universities expect incoming freshmen to have diverse literary backgrounds. Under no circumstances are students required to choose this book—or any other—from this list. Such a policy would be as despotic and closed-minded as one that forbade students from reading certain books.

Secondly ... so far, one set of parents has objected to the book. In fact, the teacher involved has received many calls of support. Of course, these supporters have done something that the *Review Atlas* has failed to do: actually contact this teacher. ...

This novel, which supposedly almost no one can understand, was on the *New York Times* best-seller list all year the year it was published and was number one for much of that time. Perhaps if the editor were to read the *whole* book, rather than just selected excerpts, he might get a more objective view.

Encouraging well-meaning people to band together to impose their values, be they literary, artistic, or moral, on the rest of society is a dangerous practice. I echo new board member Randy Brook's view: let the process go forward. I would only add to that a reminder to those who would jump on the book-banning bandwagon: there is no book that meets with everybody's approval. Whom will you select to tell you what to read?

John Van Ausdall
Monmouth

After reading John's letter, I figured he had stated clearly what a number of us teachers were thinking: why wasn't the paper speaking with all of the principal people involved in this news story? Why insult the students and parents who did understand Vonnegut? I felt John's last question certainly cut to the issue of book banning. His letter was followed by a longer reply from the editor.

> Editor's Note: There were never any references that we could find in either the story of Saturday, Dec. 2, or the editorial of Monday, Dec. 4, that anyone, other than someone who might find the topic a sore spot to begin with, could construe as an 'anti-teacher' tone. After going back over the pieces we believe that there was never such an inference given or intended, 'not-so-subtle' or masterfully so. And we certainly didn't find any mention of the 'scurrilous implication that educators in Monmouth are somehow concealing an immoral curriculum …'
>
> The problem here is, did a student in that class believe that a book, chosen from that list and OK'd by the course instructor was her assignment? …
>
> But obviously, there is at least one student who expressed "disgust" about the work and was not informed that they did not have to read this particular book. They were not told to simply return the book to the library and choose another, which would have been the logical alternative and could have avoided this entire debate.
>
> The student told the teacher that the book was "gross" much like the "misrepresentations" you accuse us of. But that didn't seem a strong enough response to the material to make the teacher understand that the child did not feel that the book was appropriate. So the teacher instead offered a "synopsis" to help

the student better understand a book she believed offensive and did not want to read in the first place.

Are we to assume from this that the teacher in question was "despotic and closed-minded," your words for someone who would make anyone either read or destroy a piece of literature? The point of this little exercise, is just what did the 15-year-old student believe? Did the student believe that the book was simply "not required" and that another novel could have been substituted, or did the youngster believe that the teacher was leaving the impression that the book was to be read? ...

Don't you think that if we were truly so "anti-teacher" and the "scurrilous" purveyors of "anti-intellectual bigotry" you portray us to be, we would have just simply identified the teacher and gone out to brew up the tar and feathers? ...

We do agree with you on one thing though. We do not believe that anyone should TELL YOU, US, OR 15-YEAR-OLD HIGH SCHOOL STUDENTS WHAT TO READ, either directly or by inference.

Oh, my God! I thought. *Tar and feathers?* This is just too bizarre to even imagine. From this point on it became obvious to me, the administration, and my fellow teachers that the local newspaper would be used to put out editorial opinions such as these. Anyone who disagreed with the editor would only encourage him to comment more strongly and more "longly." During the time the committee was meeting, the local newspaper continued to print letters to the editor, editorials, and occasional columns concerning the "book controversy."

In the midst of all this, Gary Collins once again called me to his office and asked if I could find enough copies for members of the school board to read *Breakfast of Champions*. They already had copies of my notes that Dr. Jenkins had asked me to write. The book was out of print at that point and was difficult to order. So I checked with the college, the local library, and the book stores in surrounding towns within an hour's circumference. I begged and borrowed copies and gave them to Gary to send to board members. I delivered one to Randy Brooks, the newest board member, wrapped in plain brown paper. I was wondering if the young Mr. Brooks, manager of a local grocery store, had gotten himself into more than he had bargained for in running for the school board.

While the school board members were reading copies of *Breakfast of Champions*, the media assault continued. I had to give the Kroners credit: determined to use the media outlets to influence public opinion, they did so efficiently and quickly. On the evening that the "Parents Who Care" group was meeting at the YMCA, the "parents of the victim" were interviewed on the Quad Cities ABC-affiliated television station. The Quad Cities is composed of four urban cities about forty minutes north of our town on both the Illinois and Iowa sides of the Mississippi River. A friend had called me earlier that day and said she heard a news blurb about a breaking story in Monmouth concerning a book censorship controversy, and the television station would be covering it on their five o'clock news. No, I had not been contacted for the story. However, they had contacted Gary Collins and were told they could not film inside the school. This was a school board policy.

Anxiously, I watched the interview on the news. The camera focused on the Kroners, who were seated in their living room with the thirty-eight pages of copied excerpts in their hands and their children's baby photos on the wall behind them. They explained their position much as they had done in the local newspapers. Once again, they were protecting children from a pornographic book. They used the opportunity to mention the meeting of Parents Who Care in Monmouth that evening. The interviewer's narrative explained that their student had to read the book for her high school class, and the interview included the inaccurate statement, as always, that the book was required. There was no comment from the school district other than to say that the book was being reviewed by a faculty committee whose decision would be sent to the parents.

I believe this was the point at which I was feeling the lowest. It was difficult to know whether people in the community would be supportive of keeping books in the libraries. Once you started banning books, where did you stop? Between the newspaper coverage and the television interview, it seemed that Kurt Vonnegut's book was being most brutally assaulted, and I wondered if my viewpoint would ever be requested by the media. Wouldn't you think someone would be interested in the point of view of the person who supposedly was warping children's minds? But no. Not a single person called me from the local newspaper.

A number of letters to the editor seemed to echo Mr. Stiles' point that maybe this was a book that should be taken out of the library. Anyone who wrote to the newspaper with the idea of keeping the book was treated to a long editorial reply. The exception to this rule, however, appeared to be letters from students.

The next evening, after the parents meeting, the following letters appeared in the newspaper.

From the *Review Atlas*, dated Friday, December 8, 1995:

Dear Editor:
> I am a Monmouth High School senior who is very concerned with the limited opinions of some parents in this community. If a parent does not want his or her child to read a certain book, that is one thing, but that parent doesn't have the right to tell other parents what their child can and cannot read. Second, by taking a book out of the library, you are limiting the child's education and ability to form his or her own opinions. Finally, if we are going to start removing books on the grounds of profanity and pornography, then the *Bible* is going to have to go too. For example, Judges 18 and Song of Songs (Song of Solomon) contain

passages that one might find offensive if taken out of context. If you want the next generation of children to grow up as bigots and narrow-minded people then you are on the right track. Censorship is destructive, and denies us our constitutional rights, and defies everything the United States stands for.

Thank you,
Molly Keefe
Monmouth

Editor's Note: We couldn't have said it much better ourselves. So the above letter will suffice as our comment on this topic today.

From the *Review Atlas*, dated Friday, December 8, 1995; a letter to the editor:

I am a senior at Monmouth High School, where I am very involved with literature. I have worked for the past two years on the school's literary magazine, *The Lotus*, and enjoy reading in my free time. I am also involved in journalism and am currently the Features Editor for *The Clipper*, the school newspaper. Therefore, I feel it is my civic duty to address the editorial published in the December 4, 1995 issue of the *Review Atlas*.

Foremost in my mind is the complete violation of every standard of good journalism. The editorial makes conclusions on a book after reading only excerpts of the book or knowing bits and pieces of the facts. A good journalist is open-minded, and always asking questions. However, it seems to me that the editor is particularly closed-minded on the subject.

I am also appalled to read an editorial which thoroughly insulted my intelligence. I personally read the book in question as a junior, and understood it quite well. I also did a book report on it, and received an 'A' for my work. I know several other high school students who have read the book and have no problems reading past the 'earthy language' to grasp the meaning the author was trying to get across.

Furthermore, for the past three years I have been taught by excellent high school teachers, and have been supervised by qualified administrators and principals. These individuals are more than competent to read this piece of literature and understand the meaning, theme and value of it. Monmouth High School is staffed by decidedly intelligent educators who can not only comprehend the meaning of this type of work, but have also done a remarkably fine job of teaching their students to read and interpret literature.

In response to the question about the value of this book in high school literature: this book teaches the value of making the right choices in life. I think that is a rather important lesson, and I trust that the community would agree.

I am also disappointed to see that there has been no mention of the book's theme, and so I will take it upon myself to do so. The novel discusses free will, and the responsibility of individuals to decide what is of value in our world. The author urges people to push past the 'trash' of society and to rediscover the truth of moral values. It also deals with the way people dehumanize each other by using sexist, obscene, or otherwise 'bad' language. I might also add that a reader could not identify this theme, or any other, without reading the entire novel. Even excerpts from the Bible can appear violent and pornographic when taken out of context.

The book is also a critically acclaimed piece of art. The author, in a stroke of genius, introduces himself as a character in his own book. That is a unique way of narration, which is extremely engaging to those students interested in writing.

I agree that parents should be advised as to what their child is reading. However, it is not their right to control what books are available to other students. The book in question is not required of students; that is why it is on a recommended reading list, not in actual class material. If the student was offended, he or she should have closed the book and put it back on the shelf.

From a student who cares,
Amanda Marshall

I was so thankful for both of these letters because they obviously proved what I had been saying all along: thoughtful high school students could read Vonnegut and understand his ideas.

The same night that these letters appeared in the newspaper, Ira Smolensky, a college political science professor and occasional news story writer, wrote an article about the YMCA meeting. When this censorship story broke, he found a copy of Vonnegut's novel and spent some time rereading it. From the East Coast originally, Ira had seen much of the world, read voraciously, and found Vonnegut humorous and thought-provoking. His article went far to assuage my fears that the town was agreeing with censorship.

From the *Review Atlas*, Friday, December 8, 1995:

Parents Gather to Discuss Questions Raised Over "Book"
By Ira Smolensky

If there is a broad public support for removing Kurt Vonnegut Jr.'s *Breakfast of Champions* from the High School library, it was not evident at a meeting held last night at the Warren County YMCA. While over 30 local residents attended the meeting, a majority of comments from the audience expressed fears regarding even mild forms of censorship.

The meeting was organized by Jim and Cindy Kroner, who started proceedings to have the novel removed from the library after their daughter chose it for a book report, making her selection from an English class reading list.

Mr. Kroner opened the meeting with a brief statement in which he denied that his goal was to foster 'book-burning' or 'book banning.' He also denied any personal animosity for individuals involved at the high school or in the superintendent's office.

'We are here to protect our children …… . And to elicit your support,' he said.

Mrs. Kroner then followed with a lengthier statement in which she asserted that 'our responsibility' to the author of a book exhibiting no educational value whatsoever was outweighed by that to our children.

She also cited the standard of 'sound literary quality' for inclusion in the library's collection and for class use, alleging that *Breakfast of Champions* did not in any way meet this criterion.

Mrs. Kroner closed with the following question:
'If we wouldn't want this book in our homes, why would we want it available to our children?'

After their opening statements, the Kroners passed out Xerox copies of extensive excerpts from the novel, giving the audience about ten minutes or so to look them over. Then they fielded questions.

While two members of the audience condemned *Breakfast of Champions* as 'pornography,' most of those who spoke up either defended the novel as a valuable work of literature, warned against the temptations of censorship or did both.

'By removing books, you remove choice,' one audience member asserted.

'Limiting access is censorship,' added Irene Herold, a librarian at Monmouth College.

Confronted by a number of such comments, including from some audience members who admitted that they personally would not want their children to read the book, the Kroners at first argued that they were not proposing censorship.

Mr. Kroner did say, however, that 'Maybe censorship for minors is alright.'

Clarifying their position, Mrs. Kroner said, 'We would like to not have this material available to students without parents' knowledge.'

An audience member agreed, saying that her daughter read the book the previous year, but that she [the mother] would not have given permission if she had been aware of the book's content. Asked after the meeting whether her daughter had suffered any ill consequences after reading the book, the mother said, no, but that her daughter was 'more mature than most' high school students. The woman's daughter was also present at the meeting. She defended the book and, after the meeting, said that the alleged obscenity never daunted her since 'that's not the point of the book.'

Several other issues were raised at the meeting.

To the question of whether their daughter had tried to change her assignment, the Kroners answered, 'No' but added their opinion that the burden of asking for such a change should not be placed on the shoulders of a 15-year-old.

Asked about their original request that the library's entire holdings be reviewed for unacceptable books, the Kroners did mention the possibility of instituting a review board of some kind. They did not, however, treat the idea with any visible enthusiasm.

One audience member informed the Kroners that their reproduction of such large excerpts of *Breakfast of Champions* violated copyright laws...

People who attended the meeting were a mixed group, just like the identities of the writers who had begun to send letters to the superintendent and school board. Political arguments like these often brought out "strange bedfellows." There were a number of parents from the more conservative Christian Church in the community, a few college professors, and the college librarian, and curious people who hadn't read the book but wondered what all the fuss was about. I was grateful that the community had a liberal arts college that championed freedom of speech and the right to read rather than censor books. Then, there were parents like Mrs. Shoemaker, who wanted to read the book so she could decide for herself if it was "pornographic." I believed this was exactly what Vonnegut had intended—to cause people to consider and defend their opinions.

Meanwhile the faculty committee had reviewed the book and the school board policy and issued their decision on December 11.

The high school librarian, Marilyn Black, had found that all of the "unimpeachable sources" listed in the school board's policy recommended *Breakfast of Champions* as a book of literary merit and a book that they evaluated positively for high school reading. Specifically, *Books for You*, *The Fiction Catalogue*, and *The Booklist* all reviewed the book favorably.

Mary White was a teacher in the science department, and she was no stranger to controversial issues herself. In the science field there were always ethical questions to be considered, ranging from how the creation of the earth will be taught in the high school classroom to controversy over stem cell research.

Mary White was also strongly in favor of keeping the book in the school library since it met the school board's policy regarding book choices for the library. She had the idea that a letter could be sent to parents at the beginning of each school year that explained that the responsibility for overseeing their children's reading materials resided with them. But she also felt that letter should strongly state that if a parent was concerned or offended by a reading selection, he or she should first contact the classroom teacher. Then, if dissatisfied with the teacher's handling of the situation, a trip to the principal would be warranted. This way, the complaint could be handled expeditiously and also preserve the rights of all members of the community. Perhaps it would not end up headlining the local newspaper.

The committee sent a copy of its recommendations to Gary Collins, who read the findings and agreed with them. The committee recommended that the book be kept in the library and that a team of parents and educators *not* be allowed to determine material that should be taken out of the learning centers. The decision ended with these statements:

"Standard past and present practices to this book reveal that a number of current high school students have read and understood its themes without being offended. Former students who have read this book include mainly students who have become members of National Honor Society and gone on to lead productive lives where they could make sound decisions. Some people believe that students who read this book will become 'rapists, murderers, and criminals.'

No student who has read this—that we are collectively aware of—has ended up in jail or prison."

Gary Collins recommended that the superintendent concur with the committee's findings and informed the Kroners. The following day I picked up the *Review Atlas* from the sofa where I'd flung it when I walked into the house after work. Mr. Stiles was at it again with a new editorial.

From the *Review Atlas*, December 13, 1995

> The Public's Right to Know
>
> It wasn't until the question of this particular book was raised that we discovered there is a procedure in place to handle such situations. However, now we learn that the public isn't entitled to the outcome of that procedure...
>
> ...However, no less than two media outlets, to include the *Daily Review Atlas*, were told that the school district did not have an official comment on the book ruling...
>
> The latest 'NO COMMENT' displays a rather surprising arrogance for a public body that must come to the same general public with its hand out, looking for a regular infusion of tax dollars. If you're a public enough body to require our participation when it comes to tax money and the election of a school board, then you're public enough to have to account for your policy decisions...

...The public had a right to know what the decision of the teacher's committee and principal was in this matter. And what would have been the harm to simply state that the book 'would not be removed from the school library?' There was nothing to be defensive about, except your unwillingness to own up to your decision.

We trust that if this decision is appealed, which is the right of the parents involved, we won't have to guess as to the ruling of Dr. Jenkins and/or the school board.
John R. Stiles, Executive Editor.

The local newspaper had already published a story in which Dr. Jenkins was quoted as saying the committee's decision would simply be relayed to the parents. They could decide to make it public if they so wished.

By now two weeks had elapsed since my meeting with my student's stepfather, and in that time, numerous articles, letters, and editorials had appeared in the newspapers.

Dr. Jenkins told me he had sent a letter to the family, explaining that he agreed with the committee's recommendations and would add yet an additional point. He had decided "the book" would be placed on reserve at the library and available to students who specifically requested it. They would have to sign for it, as they did for all book checkouts. It went without saying that this would keep the book from being stolen by curious students, but it would also keep the librarian constantly aware of who had the book. Dr. Jenkins did not say he would require parental permission to check out the book. I believe he felt that freedom of choice still should exist among students. He also decided to take the committee's advice and send home a letter to all parents each year that explained that they were the guardians of which books and materials their children used.

At least there was a lull in the media coverage at last, with an article in the *Register-Mail* explaining that the parents had decided to appeal the committee's decision. According to the superintendent, the next step would be to take this appeal to the board of education on January 9, 1996. So there was to be a brief respite over Christmas break in which to regroup and consider what might happen next.

On the same night Editor Stiles' story appeared in the newspaper, a meeting occurred at the public library. For several days in the *Review Atlas*, an announcement had appeared concerning a community meeting. Also, flyers had been made up by Colleen Hazen, a former neighbor, friend, and English lecturer at Monmouth College, and Tom Sienkewicz, a classics professor at the college. All of their children had been in my high school classes, and they felt a need to provide a forum for the anti-censorship proponents. I wasn't involved in the planning of this meeting, but the planners called and asked me if the committee could be there and if we would speak about the censorship issue. Their flyers looked like this:

JUST SAY "NO CENSORSHIP"

SUPPORT OUR HIGH SCHOOL TEACHERS

There will be a brief public meeting of citizens to express
support for the current Monmouth High School English curriculum
and library acquisition policies.

WARREN CO. LIBRARY
Wednesday, December 13
7:00 PM

If you do not approve of efforts to censor books like Kurt Vonnegut's *Breakfast of Champions* and to remove them from the high school curriculum and library, you are encouraged to attend this meeting. Even if you can only attend for a few minutes, your presence will show that advocates for censorship do not speak for the Monmouth community at large.

For further information
Contact ...

Obviously, I was hoping there would be a good crowd on hand to show support for the school's policies. Approximately forty adults showed up for the meeting, along with some of the high school students. The students had organized a petition, which was signed by hundreds of the high school students, that asked that the book remain in the library. The adults at the meeting also signed a petition that asked that the school board keep the book.

Finally, I had a forum in which to present my side of this issue. I was introduced after a brief description of the committee's recommendation, the principal's decision, and the possible appeal to the school board.

In part, this is what I said:

"What is at issue is the right of a group of parents to go into the learning centers and remove books they deem unfit for other people's children as well as their own. I want to make it clear that I was never approached by the complainants in this current controversy over *Breakfast of Champions*. Instead, they went to the principal and superintendent and then the media. Many of you know me and have had children in my classes. Some of you were *in* my class, and now I have your children in class. I think you understand that I would never have forced a student to read something that offended her. The first rule of common sense is to close the book and find something more appropriate. However, in this case there seems to have been a miscommunication on that issue. I never understood that the student was offended. Perhaps she should have been more specific in her concerns. Perhaps I didn't hear her correctly. Whatever she believes she told me, the message didn't come through that she found this book offensive.

"The high school library contains literally hundreds of books. Many of them written since the 1950s have offensive words, violence, and even some sexual content. Kurt Vonnegut is a well-known and much-touted author of fiction, and his books often cause controversy. I feel it would be a sad day if his books, as well as those of Steinbeck, Hemingway, Fitzgerald, Morrison, and others, were taken out of the library by well-meaning parents, causing all students to feel their absence.

"The bottom line is this: schools are supported by everyone's taxes, and they exist to serve all students. It's hard to do that equitably, but we try. For that reason, I fervently hope that you will make your feelings known to the school board members so that they will decide to keep the Vonnegut book, as well as others, in our library. Thank you."

With that Colleen asked the audience if they had questions. One lady raised her hand and asked, "Do you think this student might have caused all this commotion because she didn't have her book read and wanted extra time?"

I replied, "No, I believe the student truly did feel that this book was not one that she wanted to read, whether it was because of the content or the difficulty. I have to believe, especially as her teacher, that she was not trying to get away with a different deadline."

"Do you think because her parents objected, she should be given an alternative assignment?" she asked.

"I believe we need to protect the rights of everyone, and in this case an alternative book with a different deadline was the best way to defend her rights, too."

"What do you see coming out of this situation in the long run?"

"I believe that something really positive has come from this controversy. Our students are talking about books. So is our community. But you must remember, too, that these same students are watching to see how adults solve problems such as these in a democratic society. That's a wonderful thing."

"So if the school board rules in favor of the parents, what will you do?" the woman asked.

"I will live with whatever decision the school board ultimately makes because that is the way we operate in a school that reflects its community. I would hope, however, that you would make your views known to the board so they will realize your viewpoint is a part of this community also."

I felt so much better after this meeting. I had gotten out my point of view, and I'd explained details that had not been covered by the local newspaper. But more than that, I acknowledged that the student in this situation was a junior in high school and probably more than a bit surprised at the lengths to which this controversy had evolved. It was important to protect her rights by allowing an alternate assignment but also important to protect book choices. This I fervently believed. I could only hope that after this, the school board would agree with us.

Near Christmas break, Dr. Jenkins sent me copies of letters that the school board had received about the Vonnegut book. None of the letters was negative. While some disapproved of the Vonnegut book for their own children, they did not believe that banning the book was the way to conduct business. Some of the letters were from friends and neighbors, some from college professors, one or two from professional organizations, and some from former students.

The school board met on the second Tuesday night of each month, and in January that fell on the ninth. I attended the meeting along with fifty other people in a standing-room-only superintendent's office. Five out of seven of the board members were present, and the appeal concerning Vonnegut's book was the third item on the agenda. Prior to the board's decision, several people spoke. According to the *Register-Mail*, Craig Watson, an English professor at Monmouth College, said that "parents have a right to decide what is appropriate for kids to read, but parents should not be allowed to make that decision for others." Colleen Hazen added that if parents were allowed to decide which books would be kept off the bookshelf, "We will end up with empty shelves in the library." I also spoke briefly, but only to ask the board to keep the book in the library. The Monmouth College librarian, Irene Herold, asked the superintendent not to limit access to Vonnegut's book.

Perhaps the best description of the outcome was given by Robert Riley, school board president, in the January 10 article in the *Review*

Atlas: "Revealing that the school board received a five-page anti-censorship petition from college professors and students, Riley said sections of the community found the book's graphic passages unsavory but were unwilling to pull anything from the shelves of the MHS Media-Research Center. 'From my perspective, the community said yes, this has some distasteful things in it, but we don't think it can be legislated what is [available and what is not].'"

I was feeling very relieved—relieved that my life could get back to some semblance of normalcy, relieved that we were done reading *Huckleberry Finn*, relieved that Vonnegut's works would stay available to students who truly were intellectually able to understand them, and relieved that I felt I had conducted myself sensibly. Over the next few days, the topics of discussion over lunch in the teacher's lounge also returned to normal.

Part II

During the six weeks of debate there were letters to the editor in both local newspapers that revealed an interesting divide on the issue of censorship.

One letter that advocated censorship appeared in the *Galesburg Register-Mail*. The author deplored "how liberals have taken over our schools," resulting in "the moral decay of our youth." He felt the Vonnegut book should be "exorcised," and also a "thorough investigation" should result in getting rid of "other pornographic materials" in the high school library. Claiming to know God's viewpoint, he insisted "the godly should 'Cast out the evil.'"

The writer insisted there was a lot of trash written by authors. Pointing to H. G. Wells' *Invisible Man* and *War of the Worlds*, he cautioned that those books illustrate that "homosexuals walk among us" and also that "there is life on other planets." Both of those books he proclaimed as "blasphemous." As further proof, he offered books by John Steinbeck that teach children "disrespect and perverted sex." Danielle Steel's "sex perverted books" were also on his list of trash to throw out. Finishing the short list was *The Wizard of Oz*, which teaches us that "good witches" exist and "sorcery is okay." And this writer concluded that the high school library obviously needed a thorough cleaning of these despicable books and all others like them. I wasn't sure how to react to this letter; I think it taught me the meaning of "dumbfounded."

Following this impassioned letter came a reply that used mockery of the previous letter to defend free speech. This writer suggested a "rigorous screening" of all books, television shows, movies, music, and art. On the panel would be such experts as "Jerry Falwell, Ralph Reed of the Christian Coalition, presidential hopeful Pat Buchanan, Sen. Jesse Helms, Rush Limbaugh, Newt Gingrich, presidential hopeful Bob Dole, and Pat Robertson." He felt these "experts" proclaimed to the world their expertise on what is moral. Then he mentioned adding Hitler—if he were still alive—because he claimed to know what was morally right, too.

He rebuked those of us who are "intolerant of other viewpoints" and explained that "God gave us a brain to think with; to reason with; to use to separate the good from the bad; to use to separate the wheat from the chaff." He had a simple solution: if you are offended, close the book, turn off the music, or don't go to the movie. He explained that you decide what's right for your child in your home. "But I may not share your opinion of what's good or bad for my kids, or, for that matter, me."

After that letter—critical to the earlier one about H. G. Wells, John Steinbeck and others—came yet another letter in the Galesburg newspaper. This one chastised the previous letter writer, saying he missed the point. This writer asserted "a child's decision-making abilities are not that of an adult's." Pointing to driver's licenses, the drinking and voting age, and movie ratings, she believed such restrictions to be similar to censorship. Civilization, she emphasized, demanded that communities set the standards reflected in their schools. It's the same thing as a community's right to "regulate traffic." The parents are the ones who know what is best for their children and for that reason, she applauded "the Monmouth couple for protesting the book in question."

From the *Review Atlas*, December 19, 1995

I Remember My Days at MHS

Dear Folks,
Wow.
You know, I've been out of Monmouth for, oh…six years now. Last year, I was living in Chicago, working my collective posterior off, acting and laboring at one of the city's fine museums. The year before that, I was still in school and working in a small

village in the mountains of Pennsylvania. The year before that, I found myself in Williamsburg, Virginia.

And in all that time, good ol' Ma and Pa Lewis were sure to send me a copy of the *Review Atlas*. Just to make sure I knew what was going on.

You see, that was, and is, important to me. I know it isn't 'cool' or 'hip' to say this, but I love this town. Oh, sure, I've kind of outgrown some things—I find the big city more suited to my line of work—but I still love it. The town the people, the lifestyle that seems to prevail in this town—I find it amazing sometimes. I'm proud of my family. I'm proud of my friends.

I'm proud of my education.

I went to Monmouth High School. I was taught by the best: Mr. Van Ausdall, Mr. Pieper, and Mr. Vicare, Ms. Brokaw, Mrs. Van Kirk and many others I've forgotten to mention. All I've become is because of them, not forgetting Mom and Dad, naturally. The education I received has allowed me to pursue my dreams: I've acted in Chicago. I've gotten my Bachelors in Theatre. I even made the Dean's List at one point (God knows how.) Now, I find myself back home and working towards a Masters in Fine Arts at Western Illinois University.

And I've come home to this: Good people arguing over a book, a book I read for the same class when I was a junior at M.H.S.

Folks, it's just a book. If it bothers 'ya, then don't read it. I can understand the parent-looking-out-for-the-child thing. Good for you! You should monitor what your kid takes in. But just 'cause it's 'bad' doesn't mean those who read it will turn out corrupted and degenerate.

I look at it this way, I find Rush Limbaugh a big bag 'o wind, but I watch him. I find him the funniest thing on the planet sometimes. Every once in a while, he makes a point I might jazz with, but most of the time I find him a bit one-sided. But I watch him because it's good to know my enemy (and, I realize that's just my opinion. Don't hate me for hating Rush.) My point is this: if you are grossed-out by our friend Kurt, then write a report on what it is that offends you. Don't pass the death penalty on a book because, for example, it makes some lewd illusions to a certain water animal.

Folks, again, it's just a book. I read it seven years ago and I haven't killed anyone. As an actor, I fight this type of censorship every day—don't go there. Please. Stop this. Good teachers are hard to find. Let's not play this reindeer game.

–Adam Lewis/ Class of 1990

From the *Review Atlas,* December 18, 1995 (edited for length)

Something That Needs Considering

Dear Editor:
I followed with great interest the recent controversy over book-banning at my alma mater, Monmouth High School. It was of special interest because I have been a librarian (in public libraries) for many years and because many friends and relatives have been in the teaching profession—several in the Monmouth school system at an earlier time.

The discussion in columns, letters to the editor, and editorials was good and addressed the issues forcefully and effectively. I would only like to emphasize one point that should not be overlooked. Besides the important issue of censorship which was a legitimate concern of many writers, there is also an issue of professionalism and respect for schools and teachers.

We are in a period of 'conservative' (really reactionary) backlash that includes much distrust of social institutions, including schools. There is a great deal of demagoguery from talk-show hosts, politicians, and the 'religious right' that exaggerates discomfort over changes in society and looks for places to lay the blame.

Maybe there was no organizational agenda involved in this incident, but the call for a parent group to 'go into' the school library and take out what it considered 'trash' was a bad idea.

Parents have a right to complain to teachers and administrators. They have a right to vote or not vote for particular school board candidates or to run for school board themselves. They have a right to remove their children from a school if they can provide an alternative form of education.

They do not have the right to appoint themselves vigilante book police or in other ways to meddle in the day-to-day educational process (at least not with children other than their own.) It's foolish and a service to no one for them to attempt to do so. Perhaps those who suggested such an idea have now had second thoughts.

Incidentally, some really crude pornography, of the sort that would still probably be illegal even today, circulated among students in those supposedly more upright times. You probably can't really eliminate it, but, on the other hand, I doubt that a book by itself ever corrupted anyone. Judging the Vonnegut novel on the basis of excerpts, as one student pointed out eloquently, was incredibly unfair, which is not to say there may not be differing tastes in authors and books.

I'm proud of my hometown for having a good, intelligent fight over these issues. It's probably tough being either parents or teachers at the moment. I'm sure all the people involved in this situation are conscientious and want to do what's right.

Sincerely,
Lynn McKeown, Galesburg

These are not all of the letters, but they are a fair representation. If Kurt Vonnegut wanted to get people talking about the free exchange of ideas, censorship, and community values, he had certainly made great inroads in the heartland.

Part III

Shortly after the committee recommendation was reported, I had a most interesting phone call at home.

"Hi … ah … Mrs. Abbadusky, I wonder if I might have a few minutes of your time. My name is Shawn Gillen, and I write a column with Bill Campbell for the *Review Atlas*."

That was when I started laughing.

"*The Review Atlas*, huh? You actually are finally getting around to calling me? Gee, I wonder what this call is about."

Shawn laughed, too. "Well, it's about all the stir being caused by that book. Bill and I are writing a column for the paper, and we thought we'd give you a heads-up before we put it in."

"That's nice of you. Are you going to mention tar and feathers?"

"Well, no. We were actually going to write a piece of satire, and I thought you'd be interested in knowing that we talked to Mr. Vonnegut."

"What? You what?" I was astounded.

"Yeah. We called Mr. Vonnegut and asked him about the story," Shawn replied as if it was an everyday event.

"However did you manage to do that? I'd think his phone number would be quite confidential."

"Well, long story short … we were sitting at Bill's house talking about how the media reacted to the book story on the evening news. We considered a very simple question that no one was asking: 'What would Vonnegut have to say about this?' And Bill said, 'Wouldn't it be great if we could get in contact with Vonnegut and ask him how he feels?' I think he was only half serious when he said this. But, well, you don't really know me."

"No, I don't. Who are you besides a column writer?" I asked.

"I'm actually a student at Monmouth College. Kind of what they call 'non-traditional.' I graduated from the University of Iowa a year ago in English and am working on picking up some education hours so I can teach. You know, Kurt Vonnegut went to the University of Iowa Writer's Workshop. So I guess we have inhabited some similar geography, at least. I work with Bill Campbell who's been a reporter and editorial cartoonist for some time. Between us we put together some pretty funny pieces."

I asked, "So how did you decide to talk to Vonnegut?"

"Well, Campbell should have known that asking the question would force me to make it happen. I'm kind of a cocky twenty-four-year-old, and I figured we could just get his phone number by calling the publishing company. I went back to the college, looked up his publisher, and called them. I explained the situation and asked if I could interview Mr. Vonnegut. Of course, his interviews are handled through an agent, so I asked if I could have the agent's phone number. Amazingly, they gave it to me, and in a few minutes I was talking to him. I couldn't believe a hot-shot New York literary agent would be talking to some hick from Warren County in Illinois. But he was great. I explained what was going on back here and said I'd like to interview Mr. Vonnegut and get his take on it. To my absolute surprise, he said, 'Sure.'"

"Oh, my God! I can't believe you did that. Or that he would say 'sure.'"

"Me either. But he did. He said he'd call Mr. Vonnegut, make sure he was at home, and brief him on the situation. Then he'd give me the number, but I had to promise to destroy it after I talked with The Man. Of course, I agreed. So I hung up and a few minutes later, he called me back and told me Vonnegut was at home and expecting my call."

"How amazing! So did you have a bunch of questions put together?" I asked.

"No, that's just it. I hadn't thought it through that far. I have to tell you, I hadn't read much of his work, only a few short stories and *Slaughterhouse-Five*. I hadn't read the book causing all the commotion. But I do think pretty fast on my feet."

"And you're twenty-four, cocky, and not concerned about what the literary establishment in New York City thinks, right?"

"You got it! I dialed the number and after a few rings, Vonnegut answered the phone. It took me a few seconds to compose myself, and I told him about the situation and began to ask him questions off the top of my head. Not very good questions, I suppose, but good enough to get a few quotes for our article. I do remember one of his reactions. He asked, 'What is the last movie this girl went to? Hell, you can't watch any movies these days without hearing the word 'f—.' … Somehow I don't think Bill or I can manage to slip that word into our article."

I felt this was a great opportunity to get more information on Vonnegut, so I asked, "What was he like? What was your impression of him?"

"I picked myself up off the floor after that, and I think the best word I can think of to describe him is 'gracious.' He was very patient with me. He could probably tell I wasn't very prepared or experienced, but he treated me like a journalist. He was not a bit surprised by the controversy except over which book they were attempting to ban from the library. He was expecting it to be *Slaughterhouse-Five*. He made it very clear that book banners are breaking the law if they're trying to keep books out of libraries. And he also talked a lot about current culture and the use of expletives, violence, sex. He thinks books are pretty mild compared to what kids can see in movies and on TV."

"I'd agree with that. I imagine he found it pretty amazing that we're here in a small town in Middle America, debating this issue."

"Well, he did find it pretty typical. I think he's probably heard it all before and I got the impression that he enjoys getting under people's skins," Shawn said, and I felt he was echoing my feelings.

"That sounds exactly like what I'd expect him to say. I think that's what writers are supposed to do, isn't it?"

"Uh-huh. I'd agree. We got some good material for the article, even if I was a bit of an inept, novice reporter. And we'll probably run the column as a satire in a few days. Just thought I'd let you know so you'd expect it."

"Shawn, I can hardly pick up a local newspaper without seeing something about 'that book.'"

"Well, sells papers, doesn't it?" I could almost see him smiling.

"Sure does," I said. "Thanks for calling. I was thinking about writing to Mr. Vonnegut myself. Now maybe I will. And I'll send him a few of your editor's columns, too."

"Sounds good. Okay. Thanks for talking to me." And with that, Shawn Gillen had amazed me.

I hung up the phone and sat down to think about what Mr. Gillen had said. Maybe it would be an interesting idea to write Vonnegut via his publishing company and send some clippings from the newspaper.

My letter was dated December 12, and in it I described what was happening in our town. Before closing, I wrote:

> I have been teaching in this small town for twenty-eight years. When you were working on *Slaughterhouse-Five*, I was graduating from college at a small liberal arts school—Knox College—in Galesburg, about sixteen miles away. So we share a history of that decade with the Vietnam war, the assassinations, and so much turmoil. My father, who is seventy-five, reminded me yesterday that we come from a long and noble line of people who argue with school boards.
>
> The sad part of all this is that the world we now live in isn't much better, and is, in many ways, worse than the world of Kilgore Trout in your novel. But the happy news is that you are still causing people to think, including my high school students and their parents. I can't help but think that it is positive when so many protest censorship here in our conservative Midwest.
>
> So, thank you, Mr. Vonnegut, for enabling my students to think over these many, many years. So many of them have written about how much they loved your books.

If nothing else, please consider it a Christmas present that you still continue to get under people's skins and into people's minds and hearts.

Sincerely,
Mrs. Susan Abbadusky

Somehow mailing that letter lifted my shoulders and my spirits and explained how I was feeling about the entire experience. It was one thing to consider what various people in our small town might be thinking about my "sense of judgment," and quite another perspective to consider what the wider world might think.

Also gratifying was the following column, written by Bill Campbell and Shawn Gillen, complete with editorial cartoon:

From the *Review Atlas,* December 15, 1995

> Kurt Vonnegut, Jr.'s Heard it All Before
> By Bill Campbell and Shawn Gillen
> "What they are doing in Monmouth is as illegal as parking by a fireplug. It's breaking the law." Kurt Vonnegut, Jr.
>
> They scamper now to find a nice, cozy place in the middle, a place where they can hide, but there is no middle when you start talking about pulling books you find distasteful out of libraries.
>
> And, so, with no place to hide, they find themselves exposed as the censors they so adamantly deny they would be, with no fig leaf to cover themselves. Reasonable people rant foolish and run.
>
> Oh, no, naughty words in a book on a shelf in the high school library! Printed filth defiling and corrupting the minds of the children! Sound the alarm, obscenity is discovered!

Indeed, let there be appointed a committee! A purge must be conducted, for certainly we all agree that moral decay, wherever found, must be checked! Search and destroy!

Oh, yes, and be assured that with this cleansing there will surely come a dramatic reduction in the amount of sweating and moaning that goes on in the backseats of cars—or wherever it is that teenagers do it these days.

"So, they're at it again are they?" Kurt Vonnegut, Jr. said when told the other day that one of his books had stirred up some would-be censors in Monmouth. He did not seem surprised. At least, he didn't until we told him the book was *Breakfast of Champions*.

"Really?" he said. "That's unusual. Normally it's *Slaughterhouse-Five* they go after."

Maybe they don't have *Slaughterhouse-Five* in the library at Monmouth High School, we thought. We'll look into that, because if they don't, they should. It's a great book.

(We might even offer to buy a copy and donate it to the high school library.)

Of course, we thought *Breakfast of Champions* was a good book, too, as we were reminded when we read it again in an effort to figure out what has caused all the ruckus.

Whatever it was that was so offensive, we must have missed it.

Sure, it ain't *Rebecca of Sunnybrook Farm*, but then neither is Greek mythology with its tales of bestiality. Neither are the writings of Ben Johnson or John Donne, or Pope and the sexual implications of *The Rape of the Lock*.

"How about Chaucer?" Vonnegut added.

Scandalous, we agreed. Chaucer goes.

Of course, maybe our mistake was that we read the whole book instead of simply honing in on the excerpts. Perhaps we were snowed under by a good story told in Vonnegut's fine literary style.

Or maybe it's subliminal, we thought. Might not Vonnegut have hidden the devil in his book the way Rock musicians are accused of doing it in their songs? We tried reading *Breakfast of Champions* backwards. Still nothing.

(We did, however, find a nice recipe for tartlets.)

In fact, though it makes for great fussing and furious exchange, this talk of how we need some committee of steely-eyed, pouty-faced people rummaging through school libraries in search of smut is really, in the end, just a lot of empty noise, as Vonnegut noted.

"You know," he said, "we have laws in this country to protect freedom of expression. They say we have the right to read and write anything we want. They also say that we have the right not to read and write anything we want."

"Besides," Vonnegut added, "it's nothing compared to what kids see on TV or in the movies. You can't have a good show nowadays without using the word --," he observed.

He said he was reminded of a man in Lorain, Ohio, who called him several years ago and explained that he was a member of a parent council that was reviewing some of Vonnegut's books to see if they should be removed from the school library.

The man voted no, Vonnegut recalled.

"He told me he could learn more about sex from his fourteen-year-old than he could from the collected works of Kurt Vonnegut."

(Note to Reader: Shawn Gillen graduated from the University of Iowa in 1994 where he earned a B.A. in English. Kurt Vonnegut spent two years at the University of Iowa Writer's Workshop. Bill Campbell is a former reporter and columnist who was also an editorial cartoonist. Campbell draws better than Vonnegut. He wishes he could write even a little bit as good as Vonnegut.)

The following Monday after the Gillen/Campbell column, I was in the teacher's lounge for lunch, and I checked my mail. I grabbed some envelopes and threw them on the table while I riffled through the many sacks in the refrigerator. After sitting down, I opened my sack, grabbed my sandwich, and unwrapped it. I glanced over at the pile of mail and saw a curious envelope on the top of the pile. My address was written in bold black marker and the return address was New York City. It had an amazingly cool holographic stamp. So I opened it and began reading. About one paragraph in, I started laughing and accused the guidance counselor, Terry Miller, of playing a trick on me. He said, "I didn't. Let's see that."

Laughing, I gave him the letter and he, too, started laughing but proclaimed his innocence. Then it struck me. This was no joke. It was the real thing: Kurt Vonnegut had written me, small-town English teacher, a letter. And he'd signed it with his signature cartoon.

Jan 12 '96

Dearest (to be mildly pornographic) Susan Abbadusky --

My goodness! I would certainly have replied to your excellent letter (and accompanying materials) of December 12, 1995, long before now, if only my publisher hadn't kept it in dead storage so long. I got it today at noon!

During the past thirty years or so, I have received many letters from teachers and librarians about books by me which have caused teapot tempests or worse in their communities. You win the prize for the best one. The teacher in Drake, North Dakota, who was fired for teaching <u>Slaughterhouse-5</u>, also had his windows broken and his dog was shot. The ACLU showed up, and sued members of the School Committee personally on his behalf, and he left town with $30,000, and a glowing letter of recommendation addressed to whom it may concern. Ain't that sweet?

The censorship stories are all so <u>regional</u>. The Mason-Dixon Line still matters a lot. In small towns in Dixie, the general population is almost always solidly behind the censors and, of course, the football team. You and your students are lucky to be in Norman Rockwell America, where Jeffersonian debates are possible and usually entertaining. One community banned <u>Slaughterhouse-</u>5, and a reporter called me to find out what I had to say about it, and I said the head of the School Committee was a piss-ant, and he dropped dead the next day.

The first story of mine to arouse censors was about time-travelers who go back to the Holy Land at the time of the Crucifixion. It turns out that the Bible had it right, the three crosses, the crown of thorns and so on. As long as they're back there, they decide to measure Jesus. He is five feet and three inches tall, the same height, incidentally, as Richard the Lion Hearted. Outrage! Pandemonium!

Love you madly,

Kurt Vonnegut

By now everyone was curious about the contents. So I read it aloud and explained that the various ink globs on words were cross-outs. Vonnegut had typed it on a typewriter and used a pen to ink over mistakes. He was known to prefer a typewriter to a computer. And his merriment in describing how he had upset the system with his writing was quite obvious. He was exactly the way I thought he would be: irreverent, irascible, hilarious, and clear about his feelings concerning censorship. I was in heaven.

In short, I was overwhelmed by Mr. Kurt Vonnegut's generosity, and after that day I never failed to keep a copy of *Breakfast of Champions* in my classroom. I had his letter and envelope framed and to this day, it hangs in my living room as a reminder of what matters.

Part the Last

In the ensuing months I reflected on what I had learned from this whole tempest in a teapot. I'm sure I often hesitated and second-guessed myself when recommending books to students. My reading lists, however, never changed, and I simply updated them to keep them current.

I believe if this situation had occurred when I was a novice teacher, I would have been overwhelmed. But because I had had many years to think about what I believed, I felt instinctively that my policies were a part of my own values. Growing up in the '60s, I was open to many points of view, and this openness was always part of my teaching. While I tried not to push my own values on my students, I did believe in offering them the freedom to form their own opinions. Choosing a textbook, deciding what to teach or not to teach, recommending books, uttering challenging questions—these are freedoms to be cherished.

Mr. Vonnegut died in 2007. Prior to that sad passing, I would occasionally see him on television shows and read his latest interviews as he published a new book or spoke at a college graduation. Witty, thoughtful, challenging to the end, and always concerned with humanity and its planet, he was consistently the man of his books and his letter. I will always have a soft spot for this huge New York author who was kind enough to write a letter to a small-town English teacher. And each year in September, when the American Library Association celebrates its official "Banned Books Week," I'm occasionally asked to tell the story of "Mr. Vonnegut and Me."

Chapter Fifteen

Postscript (2008)

Rockin' Out

When I graduated from college in 1968, the notes and lyrics of the Beatles' "White Album," the Stones, Simon and Garfunkel, Grace Slick, and CCR echoed through my waking moments and stole through my dreams. My college memories included an amazing trip to San Francisco where, surrounded by the haze of pot, I watched and listened to Grace Slick and the Jefferson Airplane at the Fillmore West. (I didn't inhale, of course.) And then I remembered the midnight philosophical discussions with friends and "senior meetings" at the Broadview Hotel bar.

But now all that was over. I left my father's house for my husband's house and began life as a high school English teacher. I settled into PTA meetings, homework, car-pooling, and being "Mom" for the next twenty-seven years. Nights, I stayed up until 2:00 AM, grading English essays, feeding babies, and wondering where my free spirit had gone. It was a demanding existence that became more so eventually, because of divorce and single parenthood. In occasional, odd moments, I wondered who I had become and how I had gotten there—a tired, middle-aged mom. After child number three left for college, I spent three summers in a university town finishing an advanced degree, and there it dawned on me that in my new independence, I didn't resemble the Me of my college days. In truth, that Me no longer existed.

My children left home, married, moved away to Phoenix, and began producing beautiful grandchildren. While I flew there several times a year, "home" was still my small town and teaching part-time at the local college. Vietnam, rock and roll, and the Kennedy era—all of these now seemed like long-ago museum pieces, dusted off infrequently for visitors. Occasionally, I wondered if my students saw me as a museum piece, a relic left over from the '60s, teaching because I loved it but definitely not of their time.

On a whim, I asked one of my college students to give me guitar lessons. I had played a little in college, like everyone else in the '60s, but I had never learned to play correctly. To my utter astonishment, he agreed. Don Trinite was a kid from the Chicago suburbs, plucked out of the city and impossibly transplanted into our little patch of ground. Invariably dressed in a dark T-shirt, jeans, tennies, a small silver hoop earring, and a light green hat that read "Rolling Rock," Don sported a scruffy beard, moustache, and a perfect, white-toothed smile. A frat boy/guitar player/singer, he *was* a free spirit, something I now only vaguely recognized from my past. Three years earlier, we had struck a chord, and now he would give me lessons, and I would make him superb chocolate chip cookies, an art learned in my Mom life.

The Donald

Each week we'd meet, and he'd write down chords and teach me minor and major pentatonics. I learned a new language of fret positions, chord families, and strumming styles. He was the teacher and I the student, a stunning reversal of our relationship, and during each lesson I'd strum the chords and he'd play the melodies. He made me sound good. We fell into an easy relationship, me calling him "the Donald" and he calling me by my initials, SVK. Despite his best efforts, I was confident about being a teacher, but I had very little assurance as a musician. After several months, however, he had me feeling pretty smug. By late March, I even surprised him with a song I'd taught myself—to which he laughed, "You blow me away, SVK!"

In April my self-assurance dissolved. The Donald firmly said, "You're ready to do a concert."

"A what?"

"A concert. I think you should play a couple of songs with my ZBT band in their annual outdoor Zebestock concert."

"You know, when my kids were learning to play musical instruments, I had to leave the house because my ears hurt so badly. That's where I am on the guitar."

"Nonsense," the Donald said. "I'll fix you up with some chord progressions. You'll like it."

"In front of an audience?"

"Of course. You'll know a lot of them because they've been in your classes."

I turned pale. "That's really not something I could do."

And the Donald, self-confident, persuasive, ignoring me, responded, "Look, I know a couple of songs the band plays that you could pick up easily."

"So, I'd be a backup player, right? No more than that?"

"Of course."

Why was I worried that he didn't look me in the eye? "How exactly are you going to talk your band into this?"

"We have a meeting this week. I'll just tell the brothers we're having a guest artist. I'm in charge."

"Artist?"

He was not to be deterred. "Let's do the chord progressions and we'll see."

So we did. And I could.

The next week, the Donald said I should practice once with "the guys."

"Oh, and by the way, you'll need to play my electric guitar."

"Your *what*?"

"Electric guitar. No one will be able to hear your acoustic with the band on electric instruments."

I sighed. "I was counting on that." Then, realizing what he'd said, I added, "You have to be kidding. I've never played an electric guitar in my life."

He didn't miss a beat. "Oh, the electric is much easier to play than yours."

"But isn't it hooked to an amplifier?"

"Of course."

"I was hoping for anonymity."

"I'm tellin' ya, SVK, you can do this. Come over to the fraternity house Sunday and sit in with the guys. You'll see." I hesitated, but he was adamant. He said he'd meet me at the door at 5:00 PM.

The fraternity house. I hadn't been in a fraternity house since 1968, and they were dark and scary then. I went. Sticking my head in the door, I could see it was still dark and scary. We moved through a murky maze of hallways to a shadowy and sinister common room, where the band was set up, and four guys who were actually musicians were milling around. Their skeptical faces held polite smiles and civility. They knew I'd only had four months of lessons, but they seemed amiable. The Donald obviously had threatened them.

We played and it sounded remarkable. The songs I'd so diligently practiced were "Up on Cripple Creek" and "The Weight," recorded by the Band during the '60s. I mentioned that the tracks we were playing were laid down when I was twenty-one, and now the guys were twenty-one—a nice synchronicity. They brightened at my enthusiasm and probably were shocked that I had heard of these songs. Age has some advantages.

"I can do this."

The Donald smiled knowingly and nodded. "Thursday night. Seven-thirty."

I called my children.

These were the same children who had warned me recently that because of my small-town lifestyle, I was not to drive to Chicago because I'd probably end up in Lake Michigan and take several innocent people with me.

Mike, the oldest: "You're *what*? You have to be kidding." Then it dawned on him. "*My mom is playing in a rock and roll band?* How did this happen?"

He's the conservative one.

Jennifer, the middle: "Really? Hmmm ... that's interesting. No, Ginger, get out of the cookies. Okay, Mom. Sounds great. Let me know how it goes."

She's the multi-tasker.

Steve, the youngest: "*Fantastic!* I'll send you a shirt to wear. And you *have* to get someone to tape the performance. This I have to see!"

Ah, the last child, the one that kind of got away from me. And the shirt arrived—a black, short-sleeved tee with "The Band" on it.

May, inevitably, showed up. The night of the concert I had a bizarre schedule. A group of my friends celebrating a sixty-fifth birthday met for dinner. After that, I'd end the evening playing electric guitar in a rock band. I could see why my children were confused. I had a couple of glasses of wine for courage and dropped my car at home. Then I walked the one block to the college. I could hear heavy metal music as I ambled along because even a block away the amplifiers were thunderous, and I momentarily wondered if I could pull a stealth move and unplug mine.

Students, having heard the rumor of my probable demise, greeted me with amusement, curiosity, and giggles. One of them, Tynan, proclaimed he would be First Groupie. When the sky began to threaten with a few sprinkles, I felt vague concern about electrocution with the fatal electric guitar in my hands.

Finally, the time for our band came and I walked up to the stage where "the guys" were setting up. Picking up Don's guitar, I sat on the edge of the stage. By now it was 9:30, and the sun had been down for hours. I hadn't considered the possibility that my sixty-one-year-old eyes wouldn't be able to see the guitar strings in the dark with the stage lights behind us. I could hear my heart thudding furiously in my head and feel my wrinkled fingers shaking. The Donald smiled reassuringly and played the seven memorable notes that began "Cripple Creek." And then the Donald, Dan, Perry, Cory, Mo, and SVK played two rock songs from *my* days. No longer was I the mom/grandmother/me. I was one of the guys in the band, and we sounded amazing. The Donald sat across from me, watching my every move in case he had to call 9-1-1.

Flickering cell phone cameras taped shadowy images, and clapping and yelling accompanied us. Adolescent bodies piled on sofas moved outside for the concert, while other shadows jumped up and down. And when it ended, I experienced a sensation I hadn't felt in years: nirvana.

I glanced at the Donald, and his whole face lit up as he laughed and enveloped me in a bear hug. I hopped off the stage with new exhilaration, brought on by both adrenaline and relief. But for just a few moments I soared with the Band and remembered those days when I was Me—a free-spirited, eighteen-year-old, living day to day, with no thoughts of jobs, marriage, children, and bills. All of those years fell away and for just a moment I remembered the Me of me. And it was magnificent.

The 2008 Zebestock concert

Acknowledgments

I must gratefully acknowledge so many people whose help made this memoir happen. First and foremost is Greg Tubach, my editor at Wiley and Sons, who always encouraged me and had faith that this project would see the light of day. Thanks, patient Greg, for always being at the other end of my email or phone over these six years of writing.

The people who read these stories and made critical contributions would include Rick Kellum, Lisa Bennett, Susan Holm, Hallie Lemon, and the Faculty Writing Group at Monmouth College.

Thanks also to Jeff Rankin, who helped format the photos and verified pieces of the town's history.

Thanks to Teresa Haase Miller, who loaned me photos of the school's history.

Thanks to my daughter-in-law, Jennifer, for legal advice on intellectual property.

Thanks to my many colleagues who shared these years at Monmouth High School and who contributed to this collection.

Thanks to Megan Rakoci, Jessica Thomas, and Carrie Tinucci, former students and current public school teachers, for their great advice!

Thanks to the hundreds of students who provided information, photographs, legal releases, and encouragement.

And thank you, Karen Vandeveer, for being one of my strongest cheerleaders.

Permissions and Legal Releases

Craycraft, Bonnie West, for permission to use her photo.

Gillen, Shawn, to use his newspaper column.

Hottle, Buff, on behalf of *Portraits by Buff*, for use of senior photos, 1978–2008, and for the author photograph.

Hutton, Matt, editor of the *Review Atlas*, to use all newspaper columns quoted.

Jakoubek, Dr. Jane, to use her newsletter to the Monmouth College faculty.

Keefe, James, to use his column in the *Review Atlas*.

Keefe, Molly, to use her letter to the editor.

Lewis, Adam, to use his letter to the editor.

Martin, Tom, editor of the *Galesburg Register-Mail*, to use all newspaper columns quoted.

Marshall, Amanda, to use her letter to the editor.

McKeown, Lynn, to use his letter to the editor.

Rankin, Jeff, for permission to use his photos.

Shuler, Marianne, for permission to use her MHS photos.

Siverly, Bryan, for permission to use two aerial photos of Monmouth.

Suhor, Charles, on behalf of NCTE, to use his letter to the school board.

Trinite, Don, for permission to use his photos.

Van Ausdall, John, to use his letter to the editor.

Vonnegut, Kurt, to use his letter, identity, name, likeness, voice, signature, photograph.

CPSIA information can be obtained
at www.ICGtesting.com
Printed in the USA
FSHW02n1047260918
52549FS